THE DEATH OF ETHICS IN AMERICA

THE DEATH OF ETHICS IN AMERICA

Cal Thomas

WORD BOOKS
PUBLISHER
WACO, TEXAS

A DIVISION OF
WORD, INCORPORATED

THE DEATH OF ETHICS IN AMERICA

Copyright © 1988 by Cal Thomas.

Library of Congress Cataloging-in-Publication Data:

Thomas, Cal.
    The death of ethics in America / Cal Thomas.
        p.   cm.
    ISBN 0-8499-0638-5
    1. United States—Moral conditions.   I. Title.
HN65.T465   1988
306′.0973—dc19   88-10809
                                                                                CIP

Printed in the United States of America

8 9 8 0 1 2 3 9   AGF   9 8 7 6 5 4 3 2 1

For Dr. Richard C. Halverson
Chaplain, U.S. Senate
A man of integrity

Contents

Acknowledgments

At a time when I did not want to write another book, Dr. Jim Black of Word Books pursued me until I gave in just so I wouldn't have to take any more of his phone calls! Thanks, Jim (I think). If this is any good, you ought to get part of the credit. If it isn't, I am perfectly willing for you to accept all the blame.

Thanks, too, to McKendree R. Langley, who I first met through his marvelous book, *The Practice of Political Spirituality*, and who I have since had several opportunities to visit with in person. "Mick" contributed significantly to some of the research for this book.

My wife, Ray, and son, Jon, are due special thanks for understanding a writer's need to withdraw from contact from all living life forms in order to put words to paper (or in this case, computer screen). I hope you think the effort was worth it.

Prologue

Daily we read and hear about the moral and ethical vacuum in our country. While the nation has been preoccupied with the deadly disease known as Acquired Immune Deficiency Syndrome, another kind of AIDS seems to have become epidemic. Yet it has not prompted similarly urgent calls for a cure. This disease might be given the same acronym, AIDS, but it could stand for another malady that threatens us: acquired integrity deficiency syndrome.

Although not life-threatening in the same way as the other form of AIDS, an integrity deficiency syndrome can subtly contribute to the decline of a culture in a way that will go unnoticed until it is too late. Then we will be unable, short of revolution, to reverse the progression of the disease.

There are three primary supports that have kept

America strong and solvent: our government, our trust in God, and our free-enterprise system. These supports have been weakened in recent years by unscrupulous men and women, dedicated only to themselves. Democracy without people of character and morality will fall into disrepair and, eventually, into disrepute and anarchy.

Three major scandals seem representative. Former Senator Gary Hart's alleged sexual relationship with Donna Rice is indicative of a callous disregard for marriage and family, institutions that must be at the core of any stable society. Hart is not alone, of course, and that is the problem. He is representative of the way Americans regard adultery and—to use a nearly outmoded word—sin.

Religion has not escaped the descent into moral relativity. Though it should be the standard-bearer for believers and unbelievers, it has become as corrupt as every other institution. One editor at a major newspaper told me shortly after the news broke about Jim Bakker's sexual encounter with Jessica Hahn, "They're all alike. I don't trust any of them."

The insider trading scandal on Wall Street involving Ivan Boesky and others is a symbol of greed run amok. It demonstrates why greed is one of the "seven deadly sins" and, in fact, shows why greed can be so deadly. One of the saddest pictures I have ever seen was on the front page of *The New York Times*. It showed a dozen young men being paraded, single file, down Wall Street by the police after being charged with various violations of security laws. All were in handcuffs—a bizzare chain gang.

People with far greater minds than mine have written far greater books about ethics and morality, and this book will not supplant any of their works. What it will attempt to do is examine ethics in America from the perspective of a journalist who has both covered and commented extensively on the moral collapse.

The purpose is not to judge, for I know my own limitations. Like those about whom I write, I am a member of a fallen race. I am capable of doing the same acts, and more. It is true that "but for the grace of God, there go I."

I hope we have hit bottom with these various scandals, but I wonder at times. As Walt Harrington wrote in the 27 December 1987 *Washington Post* magazine, "Greed is the universal motive, sincerity is a pose, honesty is for chumps, altruism is selfishness with a neurotic twist, and morality is for kids and fools."

Theologian Carl F. H. Henry told me in a recent conversation, "We're in trouble as a nation. The pragmatic approach to the problems we have may seem to get things done on an obscure basis, but sooner or later the eclipse of principle will exert its toll. Pragmatism has no enduring assurance in terms of the solution it achieves. Our basic problems are not economic or political. They are moral and spiritual."

As evangelist Billy Graham once remarked, "America is not at the crossroads, as some say. America is a long way down the wrong road. She needs to come back to the crossroads and take the right road."

Part One

Providing for Common Pretense

Chapter One

Hart's Desire

When Former Senator Gary Hart announced his withdrawal from the 1988 Democratic presidential race after his reported "relationship" with a Miami woman named Donna Rice, he unbelievably asserted, "I made a big mistake, but not a bad mistake."

With this one statement, Hart revealed the wedge we have tried to drive between personal life and public life. For Hart, the mistake was poor scheduling rather than adultery.

Tragically, few questioned Hart's statement. It is sad because his remarks reveal a kind of moral retardation that cries out to be addressed.

When Hart returned to the race in December 1987, some suggested it was only to qualify for federal matching funds to pay off his campaign indebtedness. In a remarkably uncritical interview on the highly rated CBS program "60 Minutes," correspondent Ed Bradley, who promised in a promotional announcement we would see a new Gary Hart, did not challenge the newly "born-again" candidate about what may turn out to be his most outrageous assertion.

Bradley asked Hart about the pain he had inflicted on his wife, Lee, and how that had affected her support of him. Hart said that his wife was able to separate Hart, the presidential candidate, from Hart, the husband.

Whether Bradley saw the hypocrisy and inconsistency in Hart's remark, we do not know; he let it pass unchallenged.

Former Congressman John Buchanan of Alabama told me that his wife might be able to do the same thing: "If I did what Hart has done," said Buchanan, "my wife would not vote for the candidate and she would shoot the husband!"

In a television interview at Harvard's John F. Kennedy School of Government in Cambridge, Massachusetts, in January 1988, Hart again demonstrated the blurring of distinctions between morality and immorality.

In response to a question from Marvin Kalb, Hart acknowledged that he had made a "mistake, a damn fool mistake" in his relationship with Donna Rice, but he juxtaposed this statement with one about the transgressions of the Reagan administration.

"I have not broken any laws," he said. "I have not lied to Congress, and I have not shredded any papers. And we've got to get this thing in some kind of perspective."

Seeking to divorce his own personal behavior from inward character, Hart also said, "I think the task of any candidate . . . is to demonstrate qualities of character, of leadership, of courage, of independence, of integrity that are necessary not only to put forward ideas and policies but to educate the American people and to form consensus."

Hart did break the law. He certainly broke God's law against adultery, and he even broke man's law against adultery, which is still grounds for divorce in every state. Section 22-301 of the criminal code of the District of Columbia provides a fine of up to five hundred dollars and up to a year in jail for adultery, even though the law is rarely enforced. In trivializing his sexual arrogance, Hart mocked marriage, women, and the home, which are essential supports for this country.

When Hart shocked everyone by reentering the race in December 1987, he said he would no longer discuss "personal matters" because "it doesn't matter." But it does matter.

Many politicians reared on the sixties mentality of "do your own thing" are now aspiring to leadership and are demonstrating how shallow their moral water table has turned out to be. They had, like Gary Hart, deceived themselves and believed that personal morality did not matter. Now that it does matter to a growing number of people, they are left standing naked.

AN AMERICAN TRAGEDY

Even those who have helped bring about contemporary conditions, while not apologizing for their role in knocking the foundational props from under us, still view the problem with alarm. James Reston, the noted liberal *New York Times* columnist wrote, "There are theaters of violence, rebellions and uprisings of all sorts, mass hypocrisy and false sincerity fueled by television, and a general decline in courtesy and a decay of decency."[1]

The lack of any personal accountability to a moral code has made immorality respectable in our nation. There is at times little in the press, in the entertainment industry, or in our institutions of higher (lower?) learning that can lift us up or cause us to realize that we have fallen. All of the voices are coming from below, rather than from above. All of the voices call us to follow the messages from our glands.

Spies and Traitors

Recognizing the alarming number of people that have betrayed their country, *The New York Times* recounted some of those incidents in a 5 April 1987 editorial:

The spy ring run by John Walker sold technical manuals to the Navy's cipher machines and key cards to the Soviet Union. These probably enabled it to decipher millions of messages over seventeen years until 1985, leaving the Navy essentially naked to Soviet view. The theft, in the Navy's own estimation, "created powerful war-winning implications for the Soviet side." It also afforded such complete knowledge of American cryptography and communications that the security of all except totally new systems may be open to doubt.

Ronald Pelton, a fourteen-year veteran of the National Security Agency, betrayed an intelligence collection project to Soviet agents and probably his knowledge of the fifty-seven main Soviet communications signals the agency tries to intercept, one of which was at the highest level of the Soviet Government.

Edward Howard was trained by the CIA to service agents in Moscow. Fired before taking up his post, Howard later defected, probably compromising agency operations in Moscow.[2]

Although it is true that spies and traitors are not unique to the eighties (Julius and Ethel Rosenberg sold secrets of the American atomic bomb to the Soviets more than thirty years ago), such incidents now seem to occur with greater frequency. Worse, the public attention span over moral infractions seems short lived.

U.S. News & World Report published a 23 February 1987 cover story on "Lying in America" and asked whether we have become a nation of liars. It offered as proof a litany of ethical abuses including a "rash of revelations about hyped and falsified scientific research." It referred to a January 1987 study, accusing forty-seven scientists at the Harvard and Emory University medical schools of producing misleading papers. A House subcommittee estimated that in 1986 one out of every three working Americans is hired with educational or career credentials that have been altered in some way.

A U.S. News-Cable News Network poll suggests many Americans agree with John Gardner, founder of the liberal lobbying group Common Cause, who said, "Duplicity and deception, in public and private life, are very substantially greater than they have been in the past." The poll shows more than half the American people think people are less honest than they were ten years ago. Seven out of ten say they are dissatisfied with current standards of honesty—the largest proportion since 1973, at the height of the Watergate scandal.

Self-seekers and Greedmongers

It ought to alarm us that violations of ethical standards now seem to be the rule. Although it can properly be argued that, compared to all public servants, those who get into trouble are only a small percentage, that is like saying that the recent rash of airline mishaps and near collisions involve only a small percentage of all planes and passengers. This is of little comfort to the families of victims. Since we are all potentially affected by character gaps in government officials, we ought be concerned about their ethics.

Political corruption has become increasingly widespread, affecting people at the local, state, and national levels.

Last year forty-four New York municipal officials were arrested in a sting operation that involved charges of bribes and kickbacks. In another case, the former mayor of Syracuse, New York, Lee Alexander, a Democrat, pleaded guilty to charges that he masterminded a scheme that brought him $1.2 million in kickbacks from city contractors. The mayor of Washington, D.C., Marion Barry, was the subject of numerous press reports of ethical violations by himself and members of his administration, some of whom are in jail and others of whom are still being investigated.

Ex-governor Daniel Walker of Illinois pleaded guilty to fraud and perjury charges resulting in part from improper loans arranged for him from his own savings and loan institution before it went bankrupt.

An inordinate number of former and current Reagan administration officials are under a cloud because of questions involving their ethics and judgment. At the end of 1987, more than 110 senior officials had been accused of unethical or illegal conduct since Reagan took office in 1981, a number that does not include those involved in the Iran-Contra affair or the Wedtech scandal. Administration officials who have been convicted include:

- Michael Deaver, former White House staff member, of perjury.

- Lyn Nofziger, former White House staff member, of influence peddling.
- Rita M. Lavelle, former head of the toxic waste cleanup at the Environmental Protection Agency, of lying to Congress and obstructing justice.
- C. McClain Haddow, chief of staff to former health and human services secretary Margaret M. Heckler, of taking $55,330 from a nonprofit foundation he started while working for the government.
- Paul Thayer, former deputy secretary of defense, of obstructing justice and giving false testimony in an insider trading scheme.

In a scathing attack on the ethical malnutrition in government, Whitney North Seymour, Jr., the independent counsel who successfully prosecuted former White House aide Michael K. Deaver, said there is "too much loose money" in Washington and that until attitudes about ethical standards change "there is little that prosecutors can do except put a thumb in the dike."

Seymour issued a sharply worded statement following Deaver's conviction on influence peddling by former government officials. He charged that the Ethics in Government Act, which governs the contacts that former government officials may make after they leave the federal payroll, is so riddled with loopholes that it is impossible to enforce.

"Vast sums of money are on call to representatives of major corporations, defense contractors and foreign governments to buy influence and favors," Seymour said. "Much of that money is paid to 'consultants' whose stock in trade is their friendship with persons in high office. Washington money men will continue to undermine public confidence in government until lawmakers, business and community leaders and individual citizens decide to cry 'enough.'"

A small book would be required to list all the crimes committed by public officials over the last few years. The Justice Department's Public Integrity Section reported that it indicted 1,193 people in public corruption cases in 1986 alone and obtained 1,027 convictions. The section said it conducted investigations leading to indictments in 1986 of 596 federal officials, 88 state officials, 232 local officials, and 277 other people allegedly involved in crimes.

REMEMBRANCE OF THINGS PAST

Everyone acknowledges the ethical and moral collapse, including some of those who are responsible for contributing to it. Curiously, the debate is not about the problem. The debate is about how to protect one's self from the consequences of living a value-free life.

Before the doctrine of relativity superseded all other doctrines, there were people who believed that truth existed, though they might have debated its form. Today, though, few believe that truth exists except in the mind of the individual. So, what is true for one person may not be true for the other, but it doesn't make any difference as long as each person is happy. No wonder our children are confused.

Knowledge of God

The founders of our country had a concrete view of truth. Charles Perry, an Episcopal minister and provost of the Washington Cathedral in Washington, D.C., correctly observed in a *Washington Post* article for the bicentennial of the Constitution that while it does not mention the name of God, we should not forget that the document made the assumption that most people believed (or ought to believe) in God.

In a 30 April 1863 Proclamation of Humiliation, Fasting and Prayer, Abraham Lincoln said, "We have been preserved these many years in peace and prosperity. We have grown in numbers, wealth and power as no other nation has ever grown. But we have forgotten God. We have forgotten the gracious hand which preserved us in peace and multiplied and enriched and strengthened us; and we have vainly imagined, in the deceitfulness of our hearts, that all these blessings were produced by some superior wisdom and virtue of our own. Intoxicated with unbroken success, we have become too self-sufficient to feel the necessity of redeeming and preserving grace, too proud to pray to the God that made us."

When he received the Templeton Prize in Religion in 1981, Alexandr Solzhenitsyn echoed Lincoln when he said, "Over half a century ago, while I was still a child, I recall hearing a number of older people offer the following explanation for the great disasters that had befallen Russia: 'Men have forgotten God; that's why all this has happened.'

"Since then I have spent well-nigh fifty years working on the history of our revolution; in the process I have read hundreds of books, collected hundreds of personal testimonies, and have already contributed eight volumes of my own toward the effort of clearing away the rubble left by the upheaval. But if I were asked today to formulate as concisely as possible the main cause of the ruinous revolution that swallowed up some sixty million of our people, I could not put it more accurately than to repeat: 'Men have forgotten God; that's why all this happened.'"

Concept of Sin

Not only did the constitutional framers assume a belief in God, they also presupposed that human nature needed governmental control. "Madison and the framers knew about sin," wrote Charles Perry. "They shared an almost Calvinistic distrust of human conduct. In Federalist Paper No. 51, Madison writes, 'If men were angels, no government would be necessary.' But men are not angels. In Federalist Paper No. 10, Madison writes of conflicting interests that have 'divided mankind into parties, inflamed them with mutual animosity, and rendered them much more disposed to vex and oppress each other than to cooperate for their common good.'" The roots of this situation, he writes are "sown in the nature of man."

Perry continued, "The struggles of recent years are testimony to the tendency of men to usurp power. Madison and the others assumed that men are sinful and designed the system to so surround them with checks and balances that their sinful pretensions to power could not bring down the national government. Men and women have fallen from power, been removed from federal office and even gone to jail in our times because they exceeded the limits set by the framers—proving both that sin is ever with us and that the system is alive and well."

Michael Novak, a columnist and resident scholar at the American Enterprise Institute in Washington, wrote a remarkable column entitled "Ethics and Sin" (made even more remarkable by the fact that some newspapers printed it). Novak said, "It is impossible to talk about

ethics without talking about sin. Everyone of us has sometimes betrayed the moral principles we hold. No one has
lived without doing so. Still, our human weakness does
not weaken our moral principles. The principles are con-
firmed in judging where we fall short."

Novak correctly evaluated the dilemma that now confronts us over the collapse of ethics. He said, "In an age
closer to the biblical realism of Judaism and Christianity,
American leaders knew that ethics and sin are not oppo-
sites, but together. Whoever says 'ethics' says 'sin.' No
one of us makes progress without the former; and none of
us lives without the latter. For Judaism and Christianity
call human beings 'to be perfect, as God is perfect,' and
no human being ever is.

"Contemporary American discourse suffers mightily
from a loss of the concept of sin. To sin is not to violate a
taboo. It is to do, more or less deliberately, exactly what
one knows one ought not to do. Every human being
knows this experience.

"American citizens today are no more sinners than our
forebears of earlier ages; but also no less so. When we
speak of ethics, each of us may remember vividly our own
sins. Despite them, we keep struggling to do as know we
ought to do—and trust in the mercy of God."[3]

Sense of Public Virtue

A proper understanding of God and sin ought to lead
to virtue. Perry explained that an "equally important religious assumption of Madison and others among the
framers is what they called 'public virtue.' Madison
wrote, 'I go on this great republican principle, that the
people will have virtue and intelligence to select men of
virtue and wisdom.' And again he wrote, 'Is there no

virtue among us? If there be not, no form of government can render us secure. To suppose that any form of government will secure liberty or happiness without any virtue in the people is a chimerical idea.'"

Perry noted that George Washington was the embodiment of public virtue for the other founders of America. They assumed, he wrote, "that men of character would share Washington's commitment to statesmanship, allowing them to rise above self-interest and to act in the public interest with wisdom and even with courage. They believed further that those empowered to vote would be able to recognize these qualities in others. The checks and balances built into the system would serve to block the excesses of those whose public virtue did not match the demands of office."[4]

Understanding of General Welfare

Those who practice virtue will be interested in the common good of all citizens. In the Preamble to the Constitution, the founders wrote of their desire to promote the general welfare. We have twisted that language to read the promotion of everyone's welfare, which is impossible because the welfare of some may not be the welfare of others. In addition, what some think good may not be beneficial for the individual, the nation, or the world.

There is no such thing as absolute freedom. Absolute freedom is anarchy. It demands not freedom but license. Such license cannot be emotionally endured or philosophically promoted indefinitely. People crave order, so absolute freedom often leads to totalitarianism.

I debated the question of the First Amendment and freedom of speech at the University of Utah with author and columnist Nat Hentoff. Nat is a self-described "absolutist" when it comes to First Amendment freedoms. But even he acknowledges some limitations such as the necessary prohibition against crying "fire" in a crowded theater when there is no fire. He also concedes that the First Amendment was never intended to negate laws against slander and libel.

The question, then, becomes not how much freedom is to be tolerated, but what are the proper limitations for men and women who will not be restrained by an inner controller?

The answer to that question must be those restraints that promote the general welfare, provide for the common defense, and ensure domestic tranquillity. A nation's first obligation to itself and to its people is self-preservation. All of the high-sounding language in the world will not suffice if a nation disintegrates.

TALES OUT OF REASON

If our forefathers had a clear understanding of God, sin, virtue, and common good, where did the idea come from that men and nations could conduct themselves in their private and public affairs without reference to any religious values and moral principles?

E. L. Hebden Taylor, a social studies professor at Dordt College, saw the problem arising from the medieval nature-grace dualism of Thomas Aquinas that divided human life into two spheres—the supernatural, revealed to man by God's Word in the Bible, and the natural that is known to man by his own reason.

Aquinas "cut reality in two" and located the state in the natural sphere, arguing that its structure, nature, and function could be explained in purely natural or human terms.

Taylor explained, "The state was in fact the product of man's reason rather than an institution ordained by God on account of man's fall into sin, since Aquinas claimed that the fall had not ruined man's reason but only his will.

"Refusing to be directed in his thinking about government and politics by the Word of God, Aquinas instead turned to Aristotle for his political and legal doctrine. Accordingly, Aquinas taught that political institutions are an aspect of 'natural' morality, that is they can be justified on a purely human plane, independently of religious values."

No better recent example of this view can be seen than in the testimony of Associate Justice Anthony Kennedy before his confirmation by the Senate. At one of the hearings on his nomination, he said that although religious faith may be important in giving insight into a person's character, it is "irrelevant" in the matter of jurisprudence.

This view, which is widespread in our law schools and throughout American life, has given rise to the concept that the state is somehow "natural" or "neutral."

As Taylor has noted, "By dividing up human life into two realms of nature and grace, Aquinas had, of course, undermined the unified field of knowledge and experience revealed by God in the Holy Scriptures. Knowledge of the natural sphere for Aquinas could be obtained by man's reason, which had remained uncorrupted by the Fall of man into radical sin. Only man's will had fallen, not his reason."

As a result of Aquinas's view, Taylor concluded, "Man's intellect and science became autonomous or independent of God's holy Word. This autonomy, in the course of the centuries following Aquinas, was to provide the basis for the secularization and 'neutralization' of Western philosophy, law, politics, art, business life, and above all Western economics and government."

Conservative Evangelicals and Fundamentalists cannot escape responsibility for the secularization of the culture. As Taylor wrote, "Evangelical pietists [have tended] to concentrate upon the soul rather than on the structures of society, and to develop an Arminian rather than a Reformed doctrine of grace. Given such an Arminian doctrine of grace, it is not surprising that such pietists have tended, with a few notable exceptions, to think of their religion as being mainly concerned with the salvation of the individual's soul."

This emphasis on the inward by pietism, Taylor believed, "has greatly assisted in the secularization of American culture and society, since religious individualism takes for granted or ignores the structures of society outside the institutional church and seeks rather to build up significant religious cells of the 'saved' within society."

Although it would be an oversimplification to say that dualism and pietism have been totally responsible for our modern morality mess, such analyses of our philosophical roots should cause us to reevaluate our thinking and thus our actions.

LOOSE ENDS

Where has the secularization of America led us? Dr. Richard C. Halverson, chaplain of the U.S. Senate, sees the following:

Abandoning an absolute ethical/moral standard leads irresistibly to the absence of ethics and morality.

Each person determines his own ethical/moral code. That's anarchy.

Humans become their own gods and decide, each in his own way, what is good and what is evil.

Evil becomes good—good becomes evil. Upside down morality!

Good is ridiculed! Evil is dignified![5]

Topsy-turvy Values

Within weeks of Hart's pullout from the presidential race, another candidate, Joseph Biden, a Democrat from Delaware, withdrew when it became known that he had quoted from the speeches of several men without attributing the quotations and that he had flunked a law school course because of plagiarism. Biden also admitted lying about winning a full scholarship and his final academic position in the graduating class. Although he admitted his errors, in the end he blamed the system of choosing candidates for the revelations about his character.

Displaying the same sidestepping technique, former Democratic vice-presidential candidate Geraldine Ferraro seemed to excuse Hart's behavior by saying on ABC's "Nightline" that the public should forget about the Rice affair as soon as possible because "Gary is really great on women's issues."

Curiously, the debate over Gary Hart's infidelities never seemed to center on the infidelities. The "morality" of the *Miami Herald*'s methods and disclosure became more important than the candidate's views of the marriage vow.

In a commentary for National Public Radio's "All Things Considered," I spoke about the human propensity for avoiding the real issues. I said, "When I was a child and was caught breaking the house rules, I would, like other children, sometimes exaggerate in order to avoid confronting my error.

"'You don't love me anymore,' was always a good one. 'All the other kids do it,' was another. A third device was to blame someone else.

"The contemporary equivalent of this is to be found in the response . . . [of] Richard Goodwin, a former speechwriter and adviser to both Presidents Kennedy and Johnson [who] said, 'Every major political figure in this country I've known has committed adultery. We're going to end up with a man of perfect virtue and no imagination.'

"Now that is an interesting statement. Does Goodwin think that adulterous relationships help a person's imagination or does imagination help with the adultery?

"Then there is this comment by Ed Rollins, a former Ronald Reagan campaign manager and current Jack-Kemp-for-President partisan: 'Anybody out there running for president that has a skeleton in the closet ought to drop out.'

"No he shouldn't. We all have skeletons. The question is whether presidential candidates are putting new skeletons in the closet and this was the problem with Hart and Biden. The issue for both men was not what they had done in the past so much as it was what they are doing in the present. . . . The question, to borrow with attribution a phrase from my high school civics teacher, is whether they have since then 'turned over a new leaf.'"

Torpedoed Vision

In one of my newspaper columns, I remarked that "we would do well to recall Benjamin Franklin's response to the woman who asked him what kind of government the founders had produced. 'A republic, madam, if you can keep it.'

"Keeping it, so far, has been our greatest achievement. Keeping it for our posterity will be our most formidable challenge."

Today, public opinion polls, not clearly defined standards of right and wrong, have become substitutes for truth. There is no right or wrong position on abortion or foreign policy or a particular piece of legislation. There are only polls.

We are blasting away at the moral foundation of our culture, and no one seems to care. When the last supporting stone has been removed, the already burned-out structure will be a heap of rubble.

In the Broadway musical *Les Misérables,* an adaption of Victor Hugo's classic about the French Revolution, one of the songs begins as an anguished cry that echoes down through the years to our own time: "Where are the leaders of the land?"

Chapter Two

Pinkie Rings and Heavenly Things

Urgent! Open immediately!

The words on the envelope had a familiar ring.

Inside was a letter from a prominent television minister. It was dated 24 December, Christmas Eve.

Writing to me from his upstairs study, the minister said that he was about to go under financially. As if I were an old family friend, he let me know that he could not bear to ruin the Christmas of his wife and children by going downstairs and telling them the true condition of his ministry. He wondered if I could send several hundred dollars to make sure that it would be a good Christmas.

The Christmas Eve letter arrived at my house on 22 December! When I called the minister to point out that the Christmas Eve letter had arrived two days early, he replied, "There must have been a problem in the mailroom."

Another prominent television evangelist announced in an April 1982, letter that he had been chosen by God to usher in the second coming of Christ. In this letter he asked the potential donor, "Would you like to help usher in the coming of the Lord?"

A donation was required to make straight God's path.

The letter said that a ministry employee had laid a hand on the minister and prophesied, "for I have chosen you to usher in the coming of my Son."

"Electronic excitement shot through the assembly!" said the minister. "Applause burst forth from every corner of the room. I was absolutely awestruck."

So was I, especially since I happened to know the man whose agency wrote this letter. He is not even a Christian. But he is a skillful manipulator who has been used by some of the top television evangelists to raise hundreds of millions of dollars and, in the process, has become wealthy himself.

This man consistently planned "crises" for the major ministries several months prior to their occurring, meaning that he either had the ability to predict accurately the future or that he was a consummate liar and those who joined him in these lies were accessories.

If integrity, ethics, and propriety are to be found anywhere, they ought to be found in the church. Even the unchurched believe they should be able to find a standard for uprightness and virtue in the church. But the church, in the minds of many, has been corrupted by the same forces as the rest of humanity—the lust of the flesh, the lust of the eyes, and the pride of life.

SINGULAR UNACCOUNTABILITY

Public

Although most television ministers have railed against the press for their failure to understand Christians and have castigated reporters for their indulgence in stereo-type, this ignorance has been advantageous for minis-ters. It has allowed them to misstate the truth and play loose with financial statistics in a way that no business could get away with. If they were a major corporation like General Motors, their behavior would by now have been exposed.

An example may be found in a 1985 fund-raising letter mailed by a major television ministry. There are a num-ber of assertions in this letter, but none was ever chal-lenged by the press.

The letter says, "Our television agency must be paid in the next several days so that all January 1986 television station contracts can be signed. Otherwise, we will lose a major portion of our . . . TV network. . . . Over 100 radio stations have already been canceled."

Questions: How many stations' contracts were up for renewal in 1986? How many radio stations was this min-ister on in October 1985, when the letter was mailed? When were the one hundred radio stations canceled? Would the minister provide a list so that station man-agers could be contacted to verify the cancellations and the reason?

The letter says, "We need $3 million in the next few days or this ministry simply will not survive intact. We are on the verge of our worst calamity in our history."

Questions: How did he arrive at the $3 million figure? What is his current accounts payable? What was it one year ago? How many days overdue are his bills?

The letter continues, "Throughout this entire year, 1985, we have gone from one crisis to another. Militant homosexuals, abortionists, atheists, liberal politicians and the national media have conducted a campaign of 'character assassination' against me. Many of my friends have been deceived by these vicious and dishonest attacks. The result has been a major loss of financial support."

Questions: What are specific examples of campaigns of "character assassination" against him?

The letter goes on, "The national media have attempted to portray me as a fascist, a radical, and a racist."

Questions: What are some of the specific examples of how you have been portrayed as a fascist, racist, and radical? If major newspapers, news magazines, television networks, and local television and radio have given you an opportunity to present your views, do you really believe that the media are out to destroy you?

These are only a few examples of the kinds of questions that reporters ought to be asking. Since few of the major ministries are accountable to anyone, it is the role and responsibility of journalists to hold them accountable—if for no other reason than the sake of the poor and elderly who give the "widow's mite" so that these phonies can live the good life.

Industry Standards

In late 1987, the National Religious Broadcasters released a set of ethical standards by which its members would be required to abide. Although there is nothing wrong with these standards, I have three concerns. One is that the standards were drawn up by the very people they are intended to govern, ministers who contribute heavily to the support of the NRB. Would Congress allow the Executive Branch to formulate new guidelines for covert activities following the Iran-Contra investigation? Hardly.

Another concern is who will investigate charges of violations and will this person receive cooperation from those being investigated. Finally, the only penalty for failure to live up to these standards is expulsion from the organization. I seriously doubt whether any dues-paying NRB member will be expelled. We'll have to wait and see.

Contributors

The pride and arrogance of many media ministers have made them immune to the legitimate concerns and criticisms of those without a similar power base.

A contributor who wrote to a prominent evangelist in 1983 said: "I tried at least three times over the last two years by letter to explain to ____ that the fund-raising campaigns were so worded as to turn people off. I assume that a person or persons responsible for the slick insulting wording filed my letters in the wastebasket to keep their jobs secure. I am a conservative both politically and biblically and agree with every stand ____ has taken regarding such things as disarmament, abortion, homosexualism [*sic*], etc. . . . I am not a liberal critic. I tried to warn ____ that though money may be coming in by present fund-raising methods that his supporters themselves were getting disgusted with 2 to 3 requests for money per week in the mail, etc.

"Now those people have managed to give the liberal press legitimate ammunition to work with. I enclose an article [the article criticizes a fund-raising letter the minister had sent out]. What a shame to God that no one bothers to screen the fund-raising literature. . . . This is why I asked that my name be taken off the mailing lists.

"You are winning battles and getting contributions, but losing the war. I don't know if ____ is striking the rock twice or if his paid staff is using worldly means, or what?"

Staff

Enormous amounts of money, proximity to power, and the compromises many television ministers make with the truth have contributed to the crisis in which the unchurched mock the church. The problem is exacerbated because of the failure of top television evangelists to surround themselves with people who will hold them accountable, who will serve them as the prophet Nathan served David, not by ratifying fleshly attitudes, but by holding them to a higher standard.

When "people surround themselves with those who always agree, who tell them only good things," concludes Richard Champion, editor of the *Pentecostal Evangel,* quoted in a George Cornell column, "they get tripped up in public adulation. Ego takes over, and gets out of control. They see evil as something in other people, and rationalize their own behavior."

God

Powerful and wealthy ministers use God's name to ratify behavior and thinking that is clearly unbiblical, even to the person who does not go to church. It has been my personal experience that non-Christians often have a better notion of what constitutes proper and acceptable Christian behavior than do some Christian leaders. I think this is because the Christian leader has spent years rationalizing what he is doing and no longer sees the error of his ways.

The Christian leader has walked the same path he has warned his congregation not to walk. How often I have listened to sermons from pastors who warned against the first white lie, which always leads to the next lie, and the next, before you no longer realize that you are lying. There is also the warning that skipping one service or skipping one day of Bible reading and devotions gives the devil a foothold in your life. Some of these men, who began their ministries on the highest plane and with the best intentions, have long since slipped into the worst of sins, including idolatry and materialism, and they cannot even see what has happened to them.

DOUBLE STANDARDS

Men who are accountable only to themselves cannot be true to God or to other people.

The church was once condemned for preaching against sin. Now the perception among many unbelievers is that the church itself is guilty of sin. Those who have committed the sins have caused the name of Christ to be mocked just as the person of Christ was mocked on the cross and are guilty of a far more grievous sin than the drinking, smoking, dancing, and movie going they so often rail against. Like the sinners they so often call to repent, it is now their turn to repent in whatever the modern equivalent of sackcloth and ashes might be.

The trouble is that their egos have grown larger than the Goodyear blimp, and it may take a catastrophe far greater than the fall of two television "ministries" for them to realize that God does not need any of them and that his power is not revealed in greatness or bigness or growth, but in weakness.

Lying

One might paraphrase Proverbs and say that it is better for a man to have a glass of wine with dinner and be otherwise upright in his personal and financial life than to be a teetotaler and a liar. Lying is precisely what I am talking about in some of these fund-raising letters. Those who have preached about the necessity of "calling sin by its right name" ought to know that they are lying and should be told so by the public.

Greed

Following the PTL scandal and the ridicule heaped on Oral Roberts for saying that God would take his life unless he raised $8 million, the most searing indictment of television ministries run amok came in Ray Stevens's song, "Would Jesus Wear a Rolex on His Television Show?"

Woke up this morning, turned on the TV set.
There in living color was something I can't forget.
This man was preachin' at me, yeah, laying on the charm.
Askin' me for 20 with 10,000 on his arm.
He wore designer clothing and a big smile on his face,
Selling me salvation while they sang 'Amazing Grace,'
Askin' me for money when he had all the signs of wealth.
I almost wrote a check out, but then I asked myself,
"Would He wear a pinkie ring? Would He drive a fancy car?
Would His wife wear furs and diamonds?
Would His dressing room have a star?
If He came back tomorrow, there's something I'd like to know.
Can you tell me, would Jesus wear a Rolex on His television show?
Would Jesus be political if He came back to Earth?
Have His second home in Palm Springs and try to hide His worth?

Take money from those poor folks when He comes back
again?
And admit He's talked to all those preachers who say
they've been talkin' to Him?"[1]

Hypocrisy

It is easy for ministers to preach against those "sins" in
which they do not indulge such as smoking, drinking,
gambling, going to movies, and dancing. Yet what about
those ministers who refuse to deal with the sexual and
moral infidelities of their personal staff because bad publicity means bad cash flow?

If dancing, drinking, and smoking are supposed to be a
bad witness to the world (though I have yet to meet anyone who said that he became a Christian because I did
not participate in these), what kind of witness is it when
unbelievers watch ministers of the church having extramarital flings and living in splendor.

If eating meat sacrificed to idols offends my brother,
said the Apostle Paul, I will not eat meat. What if living in
million-dollar homes, driving fancy cars, and wearing of
furs and expensive jewelry leads another Christian into a
life of materialism? Will America's top preachers, who
have this rich lifestyle, stop their practices? They haven't,
yet.

Would revival break out if just one of these top television ministers followed the command of Jesus to the rich
young ruler and sold all he had, gave it to the poor, and
followed Christ? For the rich young ruler, his riches had
become his god. For too many television preachers things
matter more than God. They can talk a good game, but
unfortunately they don't know how to play it.

George W. Cornell, religion writer for the Associated Press, has noted the double standards of today's preachers. He quoted Stanley M. Burgess, professor of religion at Southwestern Missouri State University, who said about Jimmy Swaggart, "He had preached against almost everything imaginable, and then for him to do the very thing he preached against makes it all the more dramatic."

TRIPLE THREAT

Media ministers have deceived themselves, corrupted their followers, and disgusted unbelievers.

There is nothing the press loves more than a scandal, particularly when it involves impropriety by the clergy. But even more scandalous than the scores of stories written about former PTL Club president Jim Bakker's sexual dalliance with a woman from the appropriately named town of Babylon (New York), was the unseemly public dogfight among some of the top television ministers over matters that had more to do with the kingdoms of this world and who would reign over them than the kingdom of Heaven.

That the scandal may have had a greater negative impact on the unbelieving community than the positive aspects of the ministries was evident in some of the comments I have heard and read.

The editorial page editor of one of the nation's leading newspapers told me of his "utter contempt for all of them." A political cartoon by Herblock in *The Washington Post* showed dirty linen hanging on a clothesline attached to two television towers labeled Church of the Holy Antenna. The dirty linen was labeled Church of the Holy Bucks, Ministry of the Net Prophet, Ministry of Charismatic Cash, The Love-Thy-Dough Show, and Church of the Brotherly Takeover.

Syndicated newspaper columnist Richard Cohen wrote, "For some, the current scandal amounts to low comedy, a battle for bucks by a bunch of leisure-suited charlatans." (Cohen is behind the times. Few wear leisure suits anymore, having traded up to blended wools.)

William Safire, in a *New York Times* column headlined "Elmer Gantry Lives," said, "Lapses in moral rectitude will be forgiven as human vulnerability, but the blatant power-playing by preachers must dismay [their] followers and may shake their faith."

Like the drunk in the gutter, intoxication and entanglement with the world and worldly ideas about growth, power, and evading the truth have blinded television preachers to the holy and pure things of life. They no longer operate in the power of the spirit but rather in the strength of the flesh. Thinking of what might have been, of the window of opportunity that was wide open for them, and how they squandered that opportunity for short-term goals, brings me to despair.

Chapter Three

Fools and Their Money

The front page story in the Sunday, 12 December 1987, edition of *The New York Times* was headlined: "The Plunge: A Stunning Blow to a Gilded, Impudent Age." The story, by writer William Glaberson, read, "When the closing bell rang on October 19, at the end of the worst day in the history of the New York Stock Exchange, a characteristically American era came to an end.

"It was a time when 29-year-olds were earning six-figure salaries on Wall Street. Multibillion-dollar companies were bought and sold like used cars. Everybody was 'doing deals.' And stocks seemed only to go up.

"Eight weeks after the collapse, people are beginning to see that the five-year bull market of the eighties was a new Gatsby age, complete with the materialism and euphoric excesses of all speculative eras. Like the Jazz Age of F. Scott Fitzgerald in the 1920s, the years combined the romance of wealth and youth with the slightly sinister aura of secret understandings.

"'People will be looking for a point when perceptions changed,' said John R. Petty, chairman of Marine Midland Banks, Inc., who was an Assistant Secretary of the Treasury in the Nixon and Johnson Administrations. 'They'll pick Oct. 19. It will be the "ever upward and onward" being replaced by tough slogging and "one foot in front of another."'"

Accompanying what some believed to be an inexhaustible pot of gold and a never-ending rainbow was the kind of behavior that only a self-directed society could produce. It was anything but coincidental when just five weeks before the Stock Market crisis *The Wall Street Journal* carried a story in its 8 September 1987 edition with the headline: "Ethics Are Nice, But They Can Be a Handicap, Some Executives Declare."

The story reported on a survey conducted by the research firm McFeely Wackerle Jett. It asked 671 managers their views on the subject of ethics and business. The managers contended that ethics can impede a successful career and that more than half the executives they know would bend the rules to get ahead.

"I know of unethical acts at all levels of management," one fifty-year-old executive quoted in the study said. As his rationale for being unethical at times, he said, "I have to do it in order to survive."

For him, survival became the end, not honesty or truth. When such thinking becomes dominant in a culture, that culture is doomed.

The McFeely study also found that older executives generally think they are more principled than their younger counterparts. This is easily understandable given the sociological and moral upheaval younger men and women have gone through during the past twenty-five years.

The study quoted a fifty-nine-year-old vice-president at a Midwest company as saying, "Young M.B.A.'s and lawyers are taught opportunism, cleverness and cunning. Fairness and equity aren't given equal time or importance."

Perhaps most interesting of all was where these executives turn when confronted with an ethical decision. According to the survey, 44 percent consulted themselves. Only 3 percent turned to God!

No one should think that corporate America is populated with nothing but heathens. Many top executives at major corporations have not sold out to the bottom line. Tom Phillips, chief executive officer of Raytheon, and John Tests, chairman of Greyhound, are two who see beyond the profit line. Others include Sanford McDonald, chairman and chief executive officer of McDonnell Douglas; Kenneth Olson, founder and president of Digital Equipment; and Truett Cathy, the founder and president of the Chick-Fil-A fast-food chain. But, as in much of life, they are rare. The almighty dollar has supplanted the Almighty God as the object of worship—with catastrophic results.

JUST FOR A FAST BUCK

First, it is important to remember that institutions are made up of people. Capitalism itself is not evil. Wall Street alone is not corrupt. The financial community, like any other community, is only as good or as bad as the people who are part of it, and the people are as good or as bad as the educational and cultural affirmation they have received.

The Not-So-Great Society

There is a new morality today that transcends the so-called sexual revolution that AIDS and lesser concerns have brought to a screeching halt.

Unlike sex, this new morality does not even require another person. The magazines for this generation are appropriately named *Self* and *Us*.

The *Washington Post* took note of this generation's new morality in a 14 June 1987 article titled "Hopes of a Gilded Age: Class of 1987 Bypasses Social Activism to Aim for Million-Dollar Dreams of Life."

The story quoted seventeen-year-old Michelle Lentini as saying that she wanted to be a millionaire by the time she is thirty-five. "I want to be rich," she said.

Wrote *Post* reporters Lynda Richardson and Leah Latimer, "Comes now the class of 1987, a generation of new adults that many say is committed to itself with a vengeance.

"The fiery concerns of many of their predecessors over peace and social justice are momentos from a dimming past. Opinionated but not activists, troubled but resigned about political and religious affairs, the Class of 1987 . . . is gripped by a different kind of heady preoccupation."

The story continues with a quote from David Walsh, a psychologist for Fairview Hospital in Minneapolis who has studied extensively the teenage phenomenon of "designer-label kids." "We always want the best. That's carried over to our kids," said Walsh.

Although the students of the 1950s wanted what money could buy, today's graduates want it now, according to Walsh. "The inability to delay gratification is more intense because everything is more instantaneous," he said, citing television and credit cards as two examples. "If we want it, we can get it now."

Common Problems

Writing in the September 1987 issue of the American Airlines magazine *American Way,* William A. Schreyer, chairman and chief executive officer of Merrill Lynch and Company, Inc., and vice-chairman of the New York Stock Exchange, said this about solutions to the ethical crisis on Wall Street: "In seeking solutions, we've got to look at three separate elements:

"First, the human element. It's not only Wall Street that's suffered from ethical lapses. We've seen a sustained assault on traditional values for a long while now, and this has produced a widespread sense of anything goes.

"Second, we've got to examine the rules we operate by. Do they need to be tightened, or clarified, or updated? And if so, how and by whom?

"And third, we need to consider the rapidly changing nature of the financial services industry itself. With the explosion of trading volume, the proliferation of new instruments, the technological advances that link exchanges and continents, the blurred lines among the various parts of the industry, the high-stakes legal and financial battles that center on takeover attempts, the burgeoning level of debt—with all these, are we developing some new practices and techniques that invite abuse? And what new temptations are we creating that we need new protections against?"

We must agree with the first element, for without a moral foundation or universally held standards, people will abuse freedom of choice. Without rules, many new temptations are being created into which many will be led.

But Schreyer continues with a perceptive analysis of the problem of accumulating large sums on Wall Street and elsewhere. "Of all the factors contributing to what some view as the nation's decline in ethical standards, I think two have had a particularly corrosive effect: the loss of long-term perspective and the litigation explosion."

Schreyer notes that our attention span and "time horizons" have been shortened in our age and that business relationships have become "transaction oriented." In many cases, he says, "the traditional long-term relationship between a bank or a law firm and its client has given way to the business equivalent of a one-night stand.

"People who think ahead years and decades guard both their individual and institutional reputations. But to those with short-term perspective, the costs of ethical standards can seem greater than the benefits."

In many ways this is like the arguments automobile manufacturers made against the catalytic converter. The car companies said the device, designed so that internal combustion engines would release fewer pollutants into the air, would be too costly, inefficient, and ineffective. They said little about the contribution it would make to cleaner air. For many of them, the bottom line, not the upper atmosphere, was paramount.

Schreyer argues persuasively in his article that our national "litigation binge" has caused the culture to shift from a moral standard to a legal standard. "It becomes not what you should or should not do, but what your lawyers can find a loophole for. Of course, such an attitude strips social behavior of its ethical content. It sends people through life as moral neuters."

And Schreyer is on target in his proposed solution: "Some people say that we need more college courses on ethics. I doubt that anyone has been saved from sin by an ethics course. But business schools should introduce ethical considerations more consistently into case studies and into the cost-benefit calculations they teach students to make."

GREEN AND DYING

Avarice is a word we rarely hear used in a discussion or debate over our ethical dilemma, yet it perfectly describes the behavior at the root of our contemporary cultural problem. In fact, it is at the root of what used to be called "sin" before nearly everyone, including a lot of preachers and theologians, stopped using the word.

Avarice is defined as "excessive or insatiable desire for wealth or gain." Avaricious persons are completely inner-directed. They work only to please themselves, yet they are never pleased because gains only spur them to greater avarice. Their pit is bottomless because they have no foundation and no goals other than to make money and accumulate things. How depressing it must be never to be satisfied, never to be fulfilled, always on a quest without knowing the destination or when you will arrive.

As misguided as they may have been in the 1960s, the flower children, the hippies, and the rest of the left wing at least had a social agenda. They were going to change the world. They would throw off the materialism of their parents and build a better society where all would be equal and no one would go hungry or be forced to live on the street. It was impossibly idealistic, of course, but it was a goal.

Few pursue such goals today.

Rich Is Better

In his book *Greed and Glory on Wall Street: The Fall of the House of Lehman,* writer Ken Auletta offers some perceptive insights into the "value-free" generation that now controls most of the American economy. It is a chilling and often depressing picture, yet it accurately depicts our country's transition. In less than twenty-five years we have moved from a service mentality—represented by John F. Kennedy's call to "Ask not what your country can do for you; ask what you can do for your country" and the Peace Corps—to a selfish, "me-first" attitude.

"Among Americans in general," he said, "it has always been respectable to be a millionaire. What may be different today is the preoccupation even many on the left have with money. Wall Street is in; the Great Society is out."[1]

In an afterword, Auletta accurately summarizes the ethical dilemma on Wall Street and, in so doing, for much of the country.

"For the securities industry, like the Nixon administration, began by denying the rot existed. When the Levine news broke [Dennis Levine, an investment banker, pleaded guilty in May 1986, to insider trading] Wall Street reacted much as members of the Nixon administration did, insisting: *We are not crooks.* Leaders of the financial community protested that the sins of a few should not be visited on the many. Dennis Levine merely demonstrated, they insisted, that any business is afflicted with a few worms. At worst, they said, Wall Street had a Yuppie problem, a few callow youths who lacked the standards of their elders. 'I firmly believe it's an aberration, and it's happening at the fringe,' said Shearson Lehman's CEO, Peter Cohen, in July 1986."[2]

Auletta said Cohen must have been cushioned from the truth because there was plenty of evidence for anyone willing to look at it of building scandals from municipal corruption in New York and Chicago to lax ethical standards on Wall Street.

"An inspection of the Levine case would have suggested that while he was a thief, the culture or ethos of Wall Street bore at least a measure of blame."

Auletta said that during the time Levine worked at three investment banks he was alleged in fifty-four incidents to have relied on insider information to buy stock in companies about to be acquired or to make other deals. "In more than half of these transactions, neither Levine nor his employers were insiders. The implication should have been unavoidable: Levine was relying for his tips on a network of spies. His tips came from a web of people who perhaps did not think it unusual (or wrong) to peddle such information. Despite the indictments of investment bankers at three separate firms and a distinguished takeover attorney, some of whom pocketed no money but merely traded information to show off and impress superiors, the Levine case was dismissed as an aberration."

Of men like Ivan Boesky, the most infamous of those to plead guilty or to be convicted of insider trading (Boesky agreed to pay a $100 million penalty and accept a lifetime banishment from the American securities industry; he also was sentenced to prison), Auletta draws this conclusion: "They didn't comprehend that greed unbridled by tradition or caution or government restraints might induce hubris."

No Time Like the Present

Ken Auletta perfectly described the mentality of our day with Wall Street serving as his metaphor. Of those indicted so far, he says they were "greedy for the fast buck. The stock market careens up and down like a roller coaster partly because it is dominated by large institutional investors who speculate on the short-term profitability of stocks rather than invest in long-term values. . . .

"The old Wall Street, of course, had its share of scoundrels and knaves. But it concentrated more on granting conservative financial advice to corporate America and to raising capital. It did not become so enmeshed in doing 'deals.' It is instructive that in 1980 the twenty largest firms that dominate investment banking collected $10.9 billion in revenues. Just five years later, reports the Securities Industry Association, their revenues almost trebled, to $28.8 billion."[3]

Envy is what fueled much of this fire. And greed.

Auletta concluded with what ought to be obvious to everyone, and is, except to those causing the problem: "Values trickle down, not up." This is as true of Wall Street as it is for every other institution, public or private. Blaming Wall Street for the corruption of those who fell is like blaming economic conditions in the ghetto for the crime there. To do so ignores the overwhelming majority of the poor who never commit crimes.

People, like water, will run downhill, seeking their lowest level unless something interdicts them.

"The ends excuse the means," said Auletta in a reference to Wall Street that could just as easily apply to many other categories. "Conservative virtues—wisdom, caution, frugality—are not prized. Long-term loyalties—to the firm, to clients, to stocks—are often deemed inefficient. In such a climate, the most outrageous acts can be deemed normal because they are common."[4]

So Ivan Boesky, before his house of cards came tumbling down, could say in a commencement speech to graduating business students, "Greed is healthy. You can be greedy and still feel good about yourself." To this he might have added, "And you need not worry about being challenged, because success, money, and power can cover a multitude of sins."

HAIN'T THE MONEY BUT THE PRINCIPLE

On ABC's "Good Morning America," Lionel Tiger, an anthropologist at Rutgers University and the author of *The Manufacture of Evil*, asserted that modern society is indeed in an ethical crisis, a conflict created by our own wealth, but one which can be resolved.

In acknowledging that there has always been a double standard—people saying one thing publicly and behaving differently in private—Tiger said, "I think what may be new now is the very scale and intensity of our problems; that is to say, most of the ethical codes that we've created really dealt with our transition from being very small-scale hunters, gatherers, scavengers, and so on, to agriculturalists, and most of the religious systems that still operate our ethics, Judaism, Christianity, Muslim, Buddhist, and so on, emerge out of that transition from a small scale to the larger scale of agriculture and pastoralism. Now, we've suddenly shifted, really, since the Second World War, which united the whole planet in a way we had never been united before. We're now a new planet with a new scale, and those old ethics of small farmers and shepherds no longer can support the burden of getting it right."

Tiger correctly saw the problem when he said that most people living today are only two or three generations removed from agriculture and the ethical structure that supported it. Unfortunately, those who have found enterprises to replace farming have found nothing to replace the ethics by which their agricultural ancestors lived. For them, making a living and knowing how to live were inseparable. For us making a living is all we care about.

In speaking of how the Japanese have brilliantly succeeded at manufacturing quality products, Tiger noted their "quality circle," in which people who work on a product actually discuss the entire process of making it, "and it's occurred to me in dealing with this whole question of ethics . . . that what we need now in moral terms is a kind of moral quality circle, in which people who actually make a product should also have some responsibility for asking, 'Is this product necessary?' 'Is it desirable?' 'Are we scuzzy people making these?' 'Are we wonderful people?' 'How can we improve ourselves?' Or, if we don't want to improve ourselves, at least let us have the honesty of our dishonesty."

On a week-long segment on ethics on ABC's "Good Morning America," Charles Gibson, the host, turned to Michael Ruwitch, a graduate student at the Washington University Business School in St. Louis, and asked: "Isn't there a fundamental contradiction in America? I mean, this is a society that is bent on success. It is bent on achievement, it is bent on striving, and yet . . . it's supposed to be done in a moral context. But we all know that achievement in many instances requires some amoral actions."

To which Michael Ruwitch replied, "Absolutely, I think you got right to the crux of it. I mean, this is basically a bottom-line society, and just about anything is justifiable if it succeeds. Success matters. But success by what criteria?"

Richard John Neuhaus, a Lutheran theologian, responded to Ruwitch: "'Competition,' 'striving,' all the words you use, it seems to me, can be perfectly good words. It depends on what you're striving for, what you're competing for."

Gibson: "But right now, isn't the ethic to succeed materially?"

Harry Stein, a writer and creator of *Esquire* magazine's ethics column, added: "Absolutely, but there definitely should be . . . some higher moral ground that maybe you distinguish where you stop, as far as making money, or advancing your own."

Neuhaus: "Take Tom Wolfe's book *The Bonfire of Vanities*. . . . There you have your real caricature, splendidly done, of what he calls the 'Master of the Universe,' the bond players on Wall Street, you know, this guy making a million dollars a year, living in a fourteen-room apartment on Central Park West. . . . He really thinks of himself as master of the universe. This is the American story of success. And then the whole thing starts collapsing, as he has to come to terms with the reality of other people and so forth. It's a moral story; it's a moral tale. It's a morality tale that Wolfe is telling. The response of the American people to that, I think, is very, very strong, in part because they feel guilty precisely about a purely materialistic, superficial definition of success. And they recognize themselves in that."

A SMALL SACRIFICE

Responding to an article by Bob Garfield about "Yuppies," young men and women who pursue material goals often to the detriment of more meaningful ones, a *Washington Post* letter to the editor illustrated the broken lives that often result from following such pursuits.

The letter said, "I've lived both lives, Yuppie and

non-Yuppie. In the first, I was married to a professional woman and on our dual incomes we Club Med-ed,
sportscar raced, alpine skied and Kennedy Centered our
fourteen-year marriage into oblivion.

"I'm now forty-two, remarried to a woman who gave
up her 'professional' career to provide full-time care
for our one- and five-year-old daughters, and living in
Gaithersburg (Maryland) on one salary. Trips to Aus-
tralia and Europe, Saturday night dining at Nathans, and
Wolf Trap concerts are distant memories. Vacations are
now taken in our nine-year-old used pop-up camper, and
dining out means 'Hooray! Daddy's bringing home a
pizza from Piazammos.' We've just started into the second round of . . . one hundred readings of 'Pat the
Bunny' for our one-year-old. Happiness is my wife and
two restless kids picking me up at National [Airport]
after a three-day business trip. We all cry, because we are
so happy to be together again.

"Satisfaction level in my first life measured about 2 on
the 10 scale. Measured now, satisfaction is about
9.5 . . . and Bob Garfield is one of the few people who
would know or understand why."

The measure and value of a person do not consist of
the sum total of the material and disposable things he
accumulates during the course of his life. Rather it con-
sists of the level of his integrity with God, with his family,
and with those who know him.

The late philosopher-theologian Dr. Francis Schaeffer
illustrated this for me when he spoke of a giant ash heap
near his home when he lived in St. Louis. He said he
would often think that the ash heap was a monument to
the folly of fallen humanity, who work all their lives just
to acquire things that ultimately will be burned and produce a smell so putrid that no one wants to go near it.

We rarely hear such descriptions of life anymore. Self-denial is for fools or for Mother Theresa. Although we may admire it in others (for a short time, because a steady diet might produce guilt), there is no support in the culture for making a career of it.

True self-denial is not denial at all. It is the actualization of the true self. For the Christian, the real self is Christ in you. So what is really meant by self-denial in Scripture is Christ-actualization in a person's life. If we continue to identify our "self" in terms of the flesh, the struggle will be far greater to put that "self" aside. But if we begin to think of ways to feed the spirit of Christ in us, our focus will be on him and not on ourselves.

Chapter Four

Roaring Back to the Future

Like our present times, the 1920s in America was a period of ethical decline. Although it was not until 1929 that the stock market crashed, many were hammering away at the moral foundation of America even during World War I, and this would affect political, religious, and business life.

When the United States entered the "war to end all wars" in 1914, Europe had been at peace since 1815. Classic liberal scholars had viewed the absence of a general war on the Continent as a triumph for the humanistic view that people were perfectable.

When Johnny came marching home again at the end of the war, he found a different America than he had left. He also viewed himself differently than before he went to war.

When American soldiers confronted their German

counterparts, they were appalled at the unethical warfare such as the use of chemical weapons, genocidal tactics of stealing food and basic necessities from occupied territories, and unlimited submarine warfare against any floating craft, even though it might be a hospital ship or civilian vessel.

As a consequence, American soldiers saw the tenets of humanism explode on the battlefield even as the politicians at home saw President Woodrow Wilson's international peace committee, the League of Nations, unravel in the reality of a world war.

"Making the world safe for democracy," became little more than a hollow slogan in light of all that had transpired in Europe. The election of Warren Harding as president in 1920 symbolized America's disenchantment with idealism and a new desire to follow political isolationism. This attitude is what largely fueled the "roar" that became the "Roaring Twenties."

In his book *Only Yesterday,* written in 1931, Frederick Lewis Allen said of this generation that saw millions of young men transported from small towns and farms to a world and an attitude they had not previously known: "A whole generation had been infected by the eat-drink-and-be-merry-for-tomorrow-we-die spirit which accompanied the departure of the soldiers to the training camps and the fighting front. There had been an epidemic not only of abrupt war marriages, but of less conventional liaisons. In France, two million men had found themselves very close to filth and annihilation and very far from the American moral code and its defenders; prostitution had followed the flag and willing mademoiselles from Armentières had been plentiful; American girls sent over as nurses and war workers had come under the influence of Continental manners and standards without being subject to the rigid protections thrown about their Continental sisters of the respectable classes; and there had been a very widespread and very natural breakdown of traditional restraints and reticences and taboos. It was impossible for this generation to return unchanged when the ordeal was over. Some of them had acquired under the pressure of wartime conditions a new code which seemed to them quite defensible; millions of them had been provided with an emotional stimulant from which it was not easy to taper off. Their torn nerves craved the anodynes of speed, excitement, and passion. They found themselves expected to settle down into the humdrum routine of American life as if nothing had happened, to accept the moral dicta of elders who seemed to them still to be living in a Pollyanna land of rosy ideals which the war had killed for them. They couldn't do it, and they very disrespectfully said so."[1]

In the decade that followed, America saw traditional values discarded, the Judeo-Christian base discredited in the minds of millions, and the end of the old economic order in the coming of the Great Depression.

Secularization was helped along not only by the forces hostile to these values but also by the hypocrisy and discrediting of those who embraced traditional values.

Sound familiar? It should. The parallels between the 1920s and 1980s cannot possibly be overlooked.

In politics, this erosion found its worst expression in the lifestyle and policies of President Warren Harding (1921–23); in organized religion, in the Scopes evolution trial of 1925, and in the Aimee Semple McPherson "kidnap" hoax and trial of 1926; and in business, in the Great Depression that began in 1929.

As Allen wrote, "Each of these diverse influences— the postwar disillusion, the new status of women, the

Freudian gospel, the automobile, prohibition, the sex-and-confession magazines, and the movies—had its part in bringing about the revolution. Each of them, as an influence, was played upon by all the others; none of them could alone have changed to any great degree the folkways of America; together their force was irresistible."[2]

In our modern culture, the invention of the birth control pill, which eliminated a major disincentive for sex outside of marriage, the so-called liberation of women from traditional roles, the effect of this liberation on men who were no longer culture-bound to serve as providers and protectors, and the rejection by many rock stars of traditional values and their embracing of nihilism represent the contemporary triumph of irrationalism.

Even the modern "Yuppies" (young, upwardly mobile professionals) are descended from their progenitors in the twenties who entered the business market with the sole idea of making money without regard for standards or for "promoting the general welfare."

JUST POLITICS

As Gary Hart symbolizes today's value-free generation, Warren Harding epitomized his countrymen's attitudes in the 1920s.

Harding, like Hart, was a public idealist whose personal life fell far short of his expressed ideals.

A key statement on his public idealism was made in Denver on 25 June 1923: "Ours must be a law-abiding republic, and reverence and obedience must spring from the influential and the leaders among men, as well as obedience from the humbler citizen, else the temple will collapse."[3]

Harding frequently asserted that leaders as well as average Americans had a duty to set an example for upright living.

On the subject of governmental evils, Harding said they should be cured and then forgotten. In several speeches he warned his listeners not to accept the office of the presidency too rapidly since the responsibilities were very heavy. In Olney, Illinois, on 21 June 1923, he said, describing himself, the president "is just an ordinary citizen of our common country until you clothe him with authority to speak for you in government."[4]

Harding always portrayed himself in this fashion in an effort to more closely identify with the voters. In his Denver speech, Harding supported the Eighteenth Amendment, which prohibited the production, sale, or consumption of alcoholic beverages. He doubted that prohibition would ever be repealed, or at least not for many years.

The issue, as Harding saw it, was not "wets versus drys" but whether the laws would be enforced as mandated under the Volstead Act. Violations of Prohibition would cause general disrespect for the law. Said Harding, "It will bring disrepute upon our community, and be pointed to as justifying the charge that we are a nation of hypocrites."[5]

Criticizing what he termed the "new-woman" movement entering the job market at all levels, Harding upheld the traditional view of the family at Greeley, Colorado, on 25 June 1923: "Frankly, I am one of those old-fashioned individuals who would be glad if the way could be found to maintain the traditional relations of father, mother, children, and home. But very plainly these relations are in process of great modification."[6]

Harding tried to have it both ways. He stressed the

importance of the traditional role of women as home-makers while simultaneously encouraging them to enter the job market.

As the culture began to unravel in the 1920s and pressure increased on the family, Harding observed, "We need more religion, my countrymen, in our daily lives."[7] "Selfish and sordid" matters were to be rejected in favor of the "higher and finer attributes of humanity."[8]

In Seattle on 27 July, Harding again returned to this theme: "If we could have greater devotion on the part of men to the home and could better safeguard and preserve the ideals of the family relationship, then I know we would have an ample guarantee that America would become the ideal Republic."[9]

In his final words, delivered on the day he died, 2 August 1923, by his secretary, George B. Christian, Jr., at Hollywood, California, Harding wrote: "We need less of sectarianism, less of denominationalism, less of fanatical zeal and its exactions, and more of the Christ spirit, more of the Christ practice and a new and abiding consecration to reverence for God."[10]

Harding's flowery language obscured a virtually nonexistent private moral code. Its absence, in fact, was reflected in his public life as scandals forever linked to his name and administration surfaced. Perhaps the most famous were Teapot Dome, the German Metal Bank scandal, the Prohibition enforcement scandal, and the Veterans Bureau scandal. In every instance, Harding's failure to develop and live by a personal moral code led to his selection of cabinet and subcabinet officials of similar low quality who, in turn, betrayed the public trust.

In the Teapot Dome case, Interior Secretary Albert Fall, a Harding crony, leased the federal naval oil reserves at Teapot Dome, Wyoming, to Harry Sinclair and Mammoth Oil Company. He leased two similar oil reserves in California to Edward Doheney in return for a percentage, payable to the government without competitive bidding. After Harding's death it was proved that Fall accepted $100,000 in cash from Doheney and $233,000 in bonds from Sinclair.

Harding arranged for Fall to take over the naval oil reserves from the Navy Department and even approved the leasing of the lands to private interests.

In January 1923, Fall resigned to work for Sinclair's oil company after turning over the lands to those who had paid him well. Harding then tried to get Fall to accept a nomination to the Supreme Court, but Fall refused, preferring to make money in the private sector.

Fall spent 1931 and 1932 in prison and was fined $100,000 for his corrupt practices.

Another Harding crony, Veterans Bureau Director Charles Forbes, was sentenced to prison for reselling surplus hospital supplies accumulated during the war, skimming the profit for himself.

One of Forbes's more bizarre expenditures involved a cross-country drinking party. Ostensibly, the train trip was to look at twelve hospital sites. During the trip, Forbes arranged for a pool party. Everyone attended in formal attire. At the end of the party, everyone jumped in the pool, clothes and all. The taxpayers footed the bill for this spectacle.

Blinded by his own immoral practices, Harding "worked too long at doing the unessential and in trusting the untrustworthy,"[11] wrote Andrew Sinclair, a biographer of Harding.

To trust the untrustworthy, one must also be untrustworthy in one's own life. Harding was. Harding's public ideals were at variance with his real attitudes and actions in important aspects of his life. Biographer Francis Russell summed up Harding's basic religious attitude as follows: "Religion was for Harding like the Constitution, something to be honored and let alone. As a member of the First Baptist Church (of Marion, Ohio), he attended as often as a politician should, listening blankly to the sermon and shaking hands with the pastor on the steps afterward, but the religious preoccupation of his mother and brother and sisters had never touched him. There must be some reason for everything, he believed—in the odd moments when he thought about it—a God somewhere, an afterlife somehow in which one would not be judged too harshly for brass rails and poker games and the occasional midnight visits to the houses by the railroad station."[12]

Harding married Florence Kling, a divorcee, on 8 July 1891, because she pursued him and because her father was well-to-do. He did not love her; their relationship was similar to that between a bachelor and his mother—a qualified affection. Due to her illnesses and ugliness, Harding looked elsewhere for sexual release as he was used to doing. In 1905, while Ohio's lieutenant governor, he fell madly in love with the attractive Carrie Phillips, the wife of a friend. They carried on a stormy relationship until 1920 when he was a presidential candidate. He wrote her erotic love letters, which have been preserved.

Russell noted that some of these letters were shocking—full of a "pathetic eroticism." During the 1920 campaign the Republican National Committee felt that the Phillips affair was such a scandal that a way was found to give Carrie twenty thousand dollars plus a monthly sum as long as Harding was in the White House. Carrie and her husband, James, were also given a free trip around the world on the condition that they stay away from Marion, Ohio, Harding's hometown. They soon left for Japan.

Harding's second mistress was Nan Britton, who began pursuing the future president in 1914, just after she graduated from high school. Harding then began writing love letters to her. Their affair began in earnest in July 1915, and lasted until January 1923, when they last met in the White House.

During his Senate years, Harding would travel to New York City almost weekly to spend the night with her in hotels, always using an assumed name. When bored during Senate debates, Harding wrote Nan long, passionate love letters (some as long as forty pages) while at his desk in the Senate chamber. She responded in kind.

During his wife's illnesses, he often took Nan around Washington in public. Noted Russell, "Some evenings he took her to his office in the Senate Office Building and made love to her there. It was in that somewhat statutory atmosphere, late in January 1919, that she conceived."[13]

While refusing to divorce Duchess, his wife, Harding gave Nan a ring in a "ceremony" in an attempt to keep her happy. His daughter, Elizabeth Ann, was born in October 1919; he promised Nan he would see her, but he never did. From the beginning of their affair he gave her money and helped her get jobs.

With the Harding election landslide in November 1920, Nan Britton became the de facto "first mistress," although the nation at large didn't know it. But Secret Service agents, along with White House officials and orderlies, acted as go-betweens, expediting love letters, money, and pictures of Elizabeth Ann.

Shortly after the election, Nan was taken to a vacant campaign headquarters in Marion, where she met the president-elect alone. With the great election victory much on their minds, Harding with reference to their passion, remarked, "This is the best thing that's happened to me lately, dearie!"[14]

Nan visited the White House many times, and on some occasions the president made love to her in a coat closet. During one of these episodes, they were nearly discovered by Mrs. Harding, but a resourceful Secret Service agent would not let her open the closet doors, pleading "national security." A few minutes later the president was calmly working at his desk, and Nan had been whisked away. Mrs. Harding was then allowed into the Oval Office.

Nan once visited the White House on a Sunday morning, after which she and the president separately went to the Calvary Baptist Church, where she watched her lover from the balcony.

In January 1921, Nan's sister, Mrs. Elizabeth Willits, had a showdown with the president, who admitted that he was Nan's lover and Elizabeth Ann's father. He promised to provide Nan with money and Mrs. Willits and her husband with five hundred dollars monthly if they would adopt Elizabeth Ann, which they did on 15 March 1921.

The last time Nan saw Harding was in the White House in January 1923, when she pressed him about when they could be together for good and when he would recognize their daughter. He said he would look after her but was tied down until Mrs. Harding died. He pleaded with her to keep quiet about their affair because he didn't want to disappoint the Republican party and was already thinking of running for re-election in 1924.

After Harding died in August 1923, Nan unsuccessfully tried to get some additional money from the

Harding family. Then in 1927 she published *The President's Daughter,* which understandably became a bestseller.

Harding's own low moral standards were reflected in the lives of some of his senior cabinet and staff members. Attorney General Harry Daugherty gave protection to bootleggers, allowed illegal withdrawals of liquor that had been seized by the government, gave pardons for cash, and even kept President Harding supplied with liquor.

The Prohibition Bureau was riddled with corruption from top to bottom. Harding said it was "political" when Congress protested Daugherty's corrupt practices such as failing to deal with bootleggers and for making private profit by exploiting the public trust. Some top associates of the president, who made a paltry twelve thousand dollars a year, were reaping as much as twenty thousand dollars a week through influence peddling. Though Daugherty's malfeasance was the talk of Washington, Harding did nothing, becoming the butt of ridicule and derision.

Warren Harding is a clear-cut case of a person's personal moral standard (or lack of one) greatly affecting his public responsibilities and undermining the moral tone of the nation. Even if Harding had been able to carry on his sexual liaisons while at the same time appointing honorable men and women as his associates (and he did, notably Calvin Coolidge and Herbert Hoover), what does it say about a person's strength of character if he has a fundamentally weak link in his marital and sexual relationship? Does this not weaken the entire chain?

And then there's the question of fitness. A president does more than negotiate with foreign powers. He also sets a moral tone and serves as a role model for the rest of the nation. Whatever one thinks of the policies or abilities of Jimmy Carter, the fact that he went to church virtually every Sunday, held services at Camp David when he was not in town, often taught a Sunday school class, and publicly demonstrated affection for his wife, served as an important example of the kind of moral leadership that contributes to the strength of a nation.

Warren Harding's lifestyle was both a reflection of the self-directed age in which he lived and a contributing factor to that age. This is not to say that if Harding had eschewed hypocrisy there would have been less hedonism in the 1920s, though that is a possibility. But in behaving as he did, he abrogated a primary responsibility as a role model for the nation. Regardless of whatever else he may have achieved, he failed as a husband, a father, and a man. And we have the verdict on that kind of life, pronounced two thousand years ago: "What shall it profit a man, if he shall gain the whole world, and lose his own soul?" (Mark 8:36).

TRUE RELIGION

The John Scopes evolution trial in 1925 was a watershed because it dramatized the view of secularists that one cannot be both a thinker and a biblical fundamentalist.

Scopes Trial

Scopes was a public school teacher in Dayton, Tennessee. He had broken a law requiring that only the creation theory of origins be taught. Scopes was a Darwinian evolutionist. The celebrated trial featured two of the nation's best-known lawyers, Clarence Darrow for the defense and William Jennings Bryan for the prosecution.

In his memoirs, *The Story of My Life,* Clarence Darrow revealed his real intention for defending Scopes: "I was in New York not long after the arrest of Mr. Scopes, and saw that Mr. Bryan had volunteered to go to Dayton to assist in the prosecution. At once I wanted to go. My object, and my only object, was to focus the attention of the country on the programme of Mr. Bryan and the other fundamentalists in America. I knew that education was in danger from the source that has always hampered it—religious fanaticism. To me it was perfectly clear that the proceedings bore little resemblance to a court case, but I realized that there was no limit to the mischief that might be accomplished unless the country was roused to the evil at hand. So I volunteered to go."[15]

More than any other event, the Scopes trial would cause a nation to question its biblical roots, indeed the very integrity of the Bible as a source for truth. It was to serve as the final break between fundamentalists and modernists, driving the fundamentalists underground and causing them to abandon the culture. Thus, they ceded the ground to the liberals who began remaking popular education and higher learning, the law, and later the media into their own image. The consequences of that bloodless coup continue to be felt today. It is why so many conservatives find it difficult to regain their lost ground. It is easier to defend a hill from the top than to scale it from below.

Bryan's fatal mistake was his belief that he could defend the faith without any knowledge of geology, biology, or other scientific data. In this he is like many modern fundamentalists who think that quoting Scripture is sufficient to persuade those who do not accept the Bible as God's Word. Sunday school knowledge and oratory along with his considerable reputation (he had run for president three times and served as Woodrow Wilson's first secretary of state), he believed, were sufficient to win the case. They weren't. Although technically Bryan won the case, Darrow successfully portrayed him as an ignorant buffoon. Now it is Darrow who is thought to have been the ultimate victor. The mandatory teaching of evolution as fact in public schools is Darrow's legacy.

Bryan also erred in that he allowed Darrow to prosecute his own position and beliefs relative to God and the Bible. It is Bryan who should have put Darrow on the defensive, questioning the sanity of anyone who believes that such a complex and intricate yet orderly universe could simply evolve by pure chance from nothing.

H. L. Mencken of the *Baltimore Sun* reveled in the trial because it gave him another opportunity to use his poison pen to deride his least-favored group.

Mencken spoke of the people of Dayton as "gaping primates of the Upland Valleys" who delighted in "greasy victuals of the farmhouse kitchen, country smells," and "the tune of cocks crowing on the dunghill." Mencken said it was fitting that Bryan died in Dayton just a few days after the trial because he loved country people.

Said Mencken, "His place in Tennessee hagiography is secure. If the village barber saved any of his hair, then it is curing gall-stones down there today."[16]

Mencken was so antireligious, so dedicated to purging the culture of religious sensibilities, so committed to deriding the good, that he was willing to accept the immoralities and political corruption of Warren Harding and his administration. Wrote Mencken of Bryan, "He had lived long enough to make patriots thank the inscrutable gods for Harding."[17]

Mencken also said that Bryan had "lived too long and descended too deeply into the mud, to be taken seriously hereafter by fully literate men, even of the kind who write school-books."[18]

More than sixty years later, Mencken's acid critique of fundamentalists is the norm for many who do not know them. Unfortunately, there are still enough around to justify Mencken's stereotype.

Bryan's performance has become a classic example of how Christians are so often their own worst enemies when it comes to significantly affecting the culture.

The Scopes trial was significant because it further eroded the concept of an infinite personal God to whom men and women must give an account for their lives. It led inevitably to relativistic thinking with the result that the consequences of immoral behavior rather than the roots of it were constantly at the forefront. As a result, we now attempt to manage behavior rather than change it, as exemplified in today's school-based clinics.

Aimee Semple McPherson

The money and sex scandals of today's ministers are not unique; their roots can be found in biblical times and certainly in the religious life of some in the 1920s.

It is difficult for a generation, twice removed from the events of the 1920s, to understand the hold that Aimee Semple McPherson had on the nation and, for that matter, on the world. McPherson was the most prominent charismatic religious leader in America and a pioneer in radio evangelism. She was also a pioneer in using publicity long before the television age.

McPherson and her mother, Minnie Kennedy, and a secretary controlled her entire religious empire called the Echo Park Evangelistic Association. Their failure to be accountable to anyone outside their own internal, tightly knit organization sowed the seeds for eventual destruction much as the PTL and related scandals have done in the 1980s.

McPherson was the pastor of the five-thousand-member Angelus Temple in Los Angeles where she would hold forth every night of the week to a packed house and a radio audience with over one million listeners.

In 1926, at the height of her fame and influence, McPherson apparently felt a need for additional exposure. So she hatched a bizarre scheme that would give her even more fame than she could have anticipated.

McPherson concocted an outrageous scenario in which she disappeared for several weeks with her lover, Kenneth Ormiston, who was also her radio engineer, to Carmel, California, where they holed up in a seaside cottage. In May 1926, it appeared that McPherson had drowned while at the beach, but McPherson had planned a fantastic plot that Ormiston leaked to the press.

Aimee had drowned, went the story, and a massive search, lasting for weeks, was conducted along the coast. Money flowed in to Angelus Temple for a memorial fund. Later, the word was put out that she had not drowned at all (the memorial fund money was not returned!), but in fact had been kidnapped.

While she was thought to have drowned, a rumor about her body being discovered swept the country, but the body found was only that of a dead seal. Tragically, eight people died in trying to solve the mystery of Aimee's disappearance.

McPherson's supporters used the publicity joy ride to raise large amounts of money for the "ministry." When she finally surfaced, claiming that she had been abducted and had walked for days through the desert in Mexico, she conducted a "fight the devil" fund-raising campaign to raise even more money for the Angelus Temple and to pay her legal fees. She even put on a "fight the devil" pageant in which she portrayed examples through history of how the devil had battled the righteous. McPherson portrayed herself as the most recent victim of the devil's slings and arrows. There was no public accounting of how much money was raised or how it was spent.

The press ate it up. Sensational headlines added to her fame and power. During the "kidnapping" trial, she took to the radio each night to give her own perspective on the proceedings.

In 1931 the federal government sued McPherson for unpaid taxes on $169,000 raised during 1926–27 that had been listed as church income. The revenue bureau said that this sum was personal income used as legal defense fees against criminal charges made against the evangelist and therefore not related to the church. The final outcome of this case was not revealed.

Earlier, when Aimee ousted her mother from the Angelus Temple empire in 1927, Minnie Kennedy admitted receiving a settlement of $106,000 in cash and property while her daughter was left with $1.5 million, which included the Temple buildings. In 1929, it was discovered that Aimee also held $100,000 in a secret account under the alias of "Ruth and Elizabeth Johnson."

Anyone who has watched the current crop of television ministers can see parallels: the constant pleas for money, the suggestion that the devil is after the ministers, the tightly knit board of directors, the lack of accountability, the leader-prophet as sole authority, the enormous amounts of cash raised, the empire building, the arrogance, the hunger for publicity, the lack of emphasis on character development, the total commitment to numerical growth and to the bottom line as an indication of God's blessing. All of this had its beginning in the mind and work of McPherson.

Some of her other schemes included a cemetery in which the plots closer to hers cost more money, a real estate project for campers on Lake Tahoe, Holy Land tours, a movie about her trial starring the embattled evangelist, and even a plan to drop evangelistic tracts over Moscow. Although large amounts of money were donated, none of these schemes was ever completed.

The spirit of Aimee Semple McPherson lives on in Jim and Tammy Bakker. They are her direct spiritual descendants. Sadly, no one learned from McPherson's experience. Or maybe they did. They learned how to use some people's hunger for God and desire for a better world to raise millions of dollars. This money, according to initial claims from the Internal Revenue Service, accrued largely to their own benefit through exorbitant salaries and bonuses.

After the inconclusive end of McPherson's "kidnapping" trial in which she used coached witnesses, she went on a "national vindication tour" in January 1927, which, like the Bakkers' failed attempt at the same thing, sparked little enthusiasm.

After the trial and schism within McPherson's church over her dictatorial leadership, biographer Nancy B. Mavity noted, "Aimee Semple McPherson, with her instinct for the temper of the crowd, was correct in sensing a change in the public attitude. Henceforward the suspicion of scandal, the taint of publicity-mongering, hovered over all she did. The newspapers still gave her space—she was more a news personality than ever—but it was space with a difference. She was no longer, like other religious leaders and like almost all persons with very considerable wealth and public following (though she was still all these), a sacred emblem to be treated by editorial offices with careful respect."[19]

BUSINESS AS USUAL

Business, like government and religion, had sown seeds of moral destruction throughout the decade. Those seeds germinated on 29 October 1929 as the worst financial crisis in American history—the great stock market crash. Frederick Lewis Allen correctly noted that the stock market crash was not an event detached from all other events but was the final judgment on a "me-first" generation.

"Prosperity is more than an economic condition; it is a state of mind. The big Bull Market had been more than a climax of a business cycle; it had been the climax of a cycle in American mass thinking and mass emotion. There was hardly a man or a woman in the country whose attitude toward life had not been affected by it in some degree and was not now affected by the sudden and brutal shattering of hope. With the big Bull Market gone and prosperity going, Americans were soon to find themselves living in an altered world that called for new adjustments, new ideas, new habits of thought, and a new order of values."[20]

The 4 January 1988 *Newsweek* cover story was headlined, "The 80's Are Over: Greed Goes Out of Style." The story inside could as easily have served as a summation of the attitudes and events at the end of 1929. Will history repeat itself? The so-called experts say no, but the Hoover administration said the same thing in 1929 and 1930 (and Ronald Reagan's assurances following the stock market crash of 1987 sounded as if he might have borrowed from some of Hoover's speeches).

Declared President Hoover on 15 October 1929: "The fundamental business of this country, that is, production and distribution, is on a sound and prosperous basis."[21] He refused to make any statement on the stock market when it crashed a few days later.

On 19 October 1987, after the recent crash, President Reagan stated: "More people are working than ever before in history. Our productivity is up. So is our manufacturing [output]. There is no runaway inflation, as there has been in the past. I don't think anyone should panic because all the economic indicators are solid."[22]

In the early 1950s, years after his original statement of 1929, Hoover explained why he had made such a positive sounding statement: "The press insistently urged that I make a statement. Obviously, as President, I had no business to make things worse in the middle of a crash. Loath to speak of the stock market, I offered as encouragement a short statement of our progress in the productive system and the long-view strength of the country."[23]

It wasn't so much the weak economy in 1929 that did America in but rather its weak ethical base that led to all the other problems.

The parallels between 1929 and 1987, as far as the economy is concerned, are overwhelming.

In his book *The Age of Roosevelt: The Crisis of the Old Order,* historian Arthur M. Schlesinger, Jr., even praises Herbert Hoover, whom he absolves of responsibility for the crash. "He remained the most high-minded of the New Era leaders in the age of business,"[24] wrote Schlesinger, who also credited Coolidge's vice president, Charles G. Dawes, and businessman Paul Warburg with sounding the warning trumpet to a largely tone-deaf people. In his diary, Dawes wrote: "To me it seems that the signs of the coming of the present catastrophe were more pronounced than those of any other through which the United States had passed."[25]

But they wouldn't listen, even as we have turned blind eyes and deaf ears to the warning sounds that surround us today.

Schlesinger listed a number of causes for the economic and moral collapse of those times; three seem particularly relevant to serve as warnings for our current age. He wrote: "Representing the businessmen, the federal government had ignored the dangerous imbalance between farm and business income, between the increase in wages and the increase in productivity. Representing the financiers, it had ignored irresponsible practices in the securities market. Representing the bankers, it had ignored the weight of private debt and the profound structural weaknesses in the banking and financial system. Seeing all problems from the viewpoint of business, it had mistaken the class interest for the national interest. The result was both class and national disaster."[26]

As has been said, values do have consequences. A person's philosophy and world-view ultimately determine the principles on which personal relationships and public policies are established.

Part Two

Promoting the General Despair

Chapter Five

Why Johnny Lies

Thomas Jefferson, so often cited as the author of the phrase "separation of church and state," is frequently used by those who wish to mandate a secular society. Yet Jefferson listed for the citizens of his day several basic requirements for a sound education. Jefferson wrote of calculation, writing, reading, history, and geography. He wrote of a knowledge of one's rights and their exercise "with order, justice and faithfulness." And he spoke of education aiming at the "improvement of one's morals and faculties."

A 1984 Gallup Poll found that most Americans continue to agree with Jefferson. Those polled said, "Teach our children math and English and history; teach them how to learn to speak and write and count correctly; and help them develop a reliable standard of right and wrong."

In a February 1987 speech to an audience at the University of Texas, Austin, Secretary of Education William Bennett said, "If we want to improve our competitiveness, we must eventually attend to the issue of character."

Historian and twice Pulitzer Prize-winning author, Barbara Tuchman, wrote an article for the Sunday, 20 September 1987, *New York Times Magazine* called "A Nation in Decline?" (Tuchman once sent me a letter in which she strongly disagreed with a column I had written. Although we might argue over some issues, she is a perceptive thinker and an excellent writer.)

In the article she said: "Decline of a nation or a society is a provocative historical problem. In Rome, it is associated with external pressure from the barbarians and the inability of the empire's agricultural rim to offer firm resistance. In the ancient Greek cities of Asia Minor, it can be traced to the silting up of harbors, closing them to access by sea. In the Aztec empire of Mexico, it was the invasion of ruthless Europeans. In China, it is a long story.

"In the United States, who knows? One certainly feels a deteriorating ethic in many spheres. . . .

"Incompetence is a companion of decline because decline has no goal; when people do not care and have no goal in view they do not function at their utmost. They grow lax and accept defeat."

And how does she define incompetence? It is a "sloppy and ragged performance that ends in unwanted results. Competence, the obverse, is the ability to do work expertly, neatly and correctly without foolish mistakes."

Where Tuchman goes wrong, I believe, is to use this excellent opening as a vehicle to trash the Reagan administration, which, to be sure, has demonstrated some incompetence but does not hold the license for it.

When she says that "decline has no goal," she is presupposing that it is worthwhile to have a goal, and indeed it is. Nevertheless, we must be able to convince students that having a goal and being competent is something worthy of their attention and pursuit. But without a standard, a universal ethic, worthy of emulation, this is impossible.

Dr. James Dobson, the psychologist, told this story in his best-selling book *Dare to Discipline:* Some social psychologists observed a group of elementary school students on a playground around which had been erected a high fence. They decided that the fence was too restrictive and that it inhibited the ability of the children to feel free, so the fence was taken down. The children, instead of feeling free, huddled at the center of the playground, displaying evident fear of the unknown. The conclusion Dr. Dobson reached was that children need parameters. They need to be told "this far and no further. Outside of this fence there is danger. Inside, there is safety."

The surprise book of the decade has been Allan Bloom's *The Closing of the American Mind.* It is surprising because it is an intellectual book about the sorry state of American higher education, yet it topped the *New York Times* best-seller list for several months in 1987.

The subtitle of the book is its thesis: "How Higher Education Has Failed Democracy and Impoverished the Souls of Today's Students."

In the book, Bloom made a strong case that the current decline in education has been caused by a fenceless society. Bloom castigated modern education for teaching relativity, not truth. Educators, he said, no longer distinguish between right and wrong not only out of fear of lawsuits but also because they cannot. They themselves see the world through fog-shrouded glasses.

CHILDREN OF A LESSER GOD

As Josh McDowell noted in the June 1987 issue of *Eternity* magazine, "In the 1940s, according to school statistics, the three most common disciplinary problems were talking, chewing gum, and running in the halls. In the 1980s the statistics say the most common problems are rape, robbery, and assault."

According to a *New York Times* story in the early 1970s, the chief fears of a student in junior high were animals, dark rooms, high places, strangers, and loud noises. The complete cultural turnaround is evident in the fears of today's junior high students: their parents getting a divorce, nuclear war, lung cancer, pollution, and getting mugged.

Why should children (and that is still what they are, Hollywood and the record industry notwithstanding) have to be preoccupied with such earth-shattering fears when they are just beginning to grapple with their self-identity and bodily changes?

There must not be a junior high student today whose vocabulary does not include words such as "premarital sex," "condoms," "abortion," "drugs," "gay," "AIDS," and "divorce." By the time they are twenty years old, 81 percent of today's unmarried males and 60 percent of the unmarried females have had sexual intercourse. Studies show that 50 percent of today's sexually active males had their first sexual experience between the ages of eleven and thirteen.

Interestingly, studies show further that "religious-conscious girls are only 14 percent more likely to be virgins than non-religious-conscious girls."

More than 25 percent of all the abortions performed in America are on pregnant teenagers between the ages of fifteen and nineteen. Further, sexually transmitted diseases now rank as the number one reported communicable disease in the United States, with the most serious rate found in the sixteen-to-twenty age group—triple the level of the general population.

And to think that my greatest concern as a child growing up in the 1950s was how to avoid catching measles, mumps, and whooping cough.

Everyone acknowledges the ethical and moral collapse of our young people. The *New York Times* reported that "At a time of increased pressure from top federal officials and some educators and parents groups for public schools to teach moral values, many educators in the New York area say they deliberately avoid trying to tell students what is ethically right and wrong."

Imagine!

And what kind of student has such an approach produced? The kind taught by psychology teacher Gary Tankard of Teaneck, New Jersey.

Tankard led twenty-six high school juniors and seniors through a class on the kinds of tests used to detect personality disorders. Jonathan Friendly, reporting Tankard's findings in the 2 December 1985 edition of *The New York Times,* said that the students have come to believe that faith in God is to be included in the category of "personality disorders." Tankard does nothing to discourage such a view. In fact, he promotes it.

Questions on one test measure possibly unhealthy religious convictions and ask students to cite examples of unhealthy beliefs.

"Even in this school there are people who are, like, fanatics," said Donna Williams, one of the students. "They say if you're not born again, if you're not saved, you are going to hell. That really scares you."

And well it should, but not for the reasons Tankard thinks. That this has been the message of the Christian church since its founding escapes both Tankard and the newspaper reporter. It is as if the idea of being born again is a cultish fad created by a deranged individual who lives in a remote South American jungle rather than the central teaching of Jesus Christ.

Yes, agreed another student, Anne Marie Mueller, "people take the Bible too literally." We all know what taking the Bible literally means, don't we? That means you believe in the miracles and in everything that science, the real god of our culture and of many teachers, cannot explain. But just because the Bible says we are to be the salt of the earth doesn't mean that literalists are all made out of sodium chloride!

Tankard, in an attempt to keep the test from becoming a complete bore, says he had in mind cults, such as the people who drank cyanide-laced Kool-Aid at Jonestown, Guyana. But the students never waivered.

"Absolutely," interjected another student, Gordon Chambers, "and how about those Sunday morning television evangelists? They tell you to give up everything you own," he said. "It's dangerous when people think they don't have a life except in the church."

So we have quickly moved from Jim Jones, persuading people to kill themselves with poisoned Kool-Aid, to ministers who use television to preach the gospel (none of whom tell you to give up everything you own), and finally to people who place the church at the center of their lives. All who believe in anything higher than money, the state, and NFL football are in for a lot of condemnation by this class.

CHILDREN OF YESTERDAY

It has not always been this way, but the longer we allow it to continue, the more our memories will fade.

The National Education Association (NEA) is the chief education lobby responsible for kicking out the props that once supported the best of American public education.

In 1941, the NEA published *The American Citizens Handbook.* In that handbook, the NEA detailed its view of what constituted a good citizen and what children ought to be taught to become good citizens. The NEA has changed radically. The principles remain valid and worth reconsideration.

World War II sharpened the organization's sense of the importance of America's freedoms and what was necessary to preserve them.

On page 36 of the *Handbook,* we find in an essay written by a former college professor, an unapologetic affirmation of where our strength as a nation comes from:

We have a military preparedness challenge to face on a national front. We hope and expect that this is being given proper attention. This is the responsibility of professionals in another field. Shall we (educators), in our own professional bailiwick, do our job in the field of intellectual and moral preparedness so that this democracy shall have unity, a national goal, and a loyal citizenship which believes that law, equality and justice are worthy of any necessary sacrifice?

This is a clearly defined goal of where we, as a nation, ought to be heading. The *Handbook's* recommendations for the methods that ought to be used to ensure we get there are no less specific. In an essay by a former chief justice of the Supreme Court entitled "What the Flag Means," he wrote:

> It means America first; it means an undivided allegiance. . . . It means that you cannot be saved by the valor and devotion of your ancestors; that to each generation comes its patriotic duty; and that upon your willingness to sacrifice and endure as those before you have sacrificed and endured rests the national hope.
>
> It speaks of equal rights; of the inspiration of free institutions exemplified and vindicated; of liberty under law intelligently conceived and impartially administered. There is not a thread in it but scorns self-indulgence, weakness, and rapacity. It is eloquent of our common destiny.

A recent survey by the American Federation of Teachers and the National Endowment for the Humanities faulted public schools for failing to teach our children about the values and virtues of democracy. It goes without saying that communist nations teach *their* children about what they regard as the virtues of their philosophy. Yet we seem reticent to do the same with our own system.

The *NEA Handbook* of 1941 says in part five, in a section called "Charters of American Democracy," that the texts of certain documents ought to be fundamental to the appreciation of the democratic way of life. They include the Magna Charta, the Mayflower Compact (avoided in most schools because of its strong religious flavor and frequent references to God), the Declaration of Independence, Washington's Farewell Address, the

Gettysburg Address, Lincoln's Second Inaugural Address, and the Constitution of the United States.

About the Constitution it said: "Every American should know its content. It is the greatest single document in the entire struggle of mankind for orderly self-government."

What was the origin of the ideas for the Constitution? Did they evolve as humankind is supposed to have done? In a section on "Religious Ideals, the Foundation," the *Handbook* answers that question:

> The American concept of democracy in government had its roots in religious belief. This ideal of the brotherhood of man roots down into the fundamentals of religion. The teachings of the Hebrew Prophets and of Jesus Christ inculcate the idea of brotherhood. The growth of the idea gave us the concept of democracy in government. It ennobled home life. It emphasized the sacredness of human personality.

Try teaching that concept in any public school in America in 1988 and you risk being fired. Yet in 1941, the NEA properly saw this as the foundation of a nation and of all higher education.

And *The American Citizens Handbook* contains the texts of a few documents it found were indispensable to an understanding of the Judeo-Christian tradition. They include the Golden Rule, the Ten Commandments (banned in our time from display in Kentucky public schools because the court found they violate church-state separation), the Lord's Prayer, and 1 Corinthians 13.

Today what passes for education is nothing more than moral relativism.

What did the NEA of forty-seven years ago think was the proper way to go about teaching patriotism to young people? In part two, "Patriotic Selections, Poetry, and Song," the *Handbook* tells us:

> I believe in the United States of America as a government of the people, by the people, for the people, whose just powers are derived from the consent of the governed; a democracy in a republic; a sovereign nation of many sovereign states; a perfect union, one and inseparable, established upon those principles of freedom, equality, justice, and humanity for which American patriots sacrificed their lives and fortunes.
>
> I therefore believe it is my duty to my country to love it, to support its Constitution, to obey its laws, to respect its flag, and to defend it against all enemies.

This is not indoctrination but inculcation of love for country. And how should we approach these truths? The *Handbook* sets the appropriate tone in an essay written by a former Executive Secretary of the NEA:

> I thank God I'm an American. All may not be right with America. There is still with us some of the social injustice and inequality to the removal of which we dedicated ourselves as a young nation. But the fundamental human rights which are the essence of Americanism are still held sacred by our people and by our responsible leaders. We have all and much more than the Pilgrim fathers expected to secure for their posterity in the New World.

In the same essay, there is this reminder that certain forms of government cannot be morally sanctioned. It is a stern rebuke to modernists who believe in a doctrine of what has come to be known as "moral equivalency." Said the *Handbook:*

> I am glad to have these rights guaranteed to me in the most sacred instrument of our government—the fundamental

law of the land—so they cannot be taken from me by pretext or annulled at the will of some dictator. I count it one of the greatest blessings that I can exercise these rights without fear of secret police, concentration camps, or exile from my country.

What about "values," a subject that seems to dominate our culture today. Values were self-evident truths two generations ago in the sense that not only did virtually everyone expect that values would be taught, they also knew which values they wanted taught. It was these values that produced the kinds of citizens the country believed would "promote the general welfare, provide for the common defense, and insure domestic tranquility." In part one, right at the beginning of the *NEA Handbook*, a section on "The Code of the Good American" was laid out for all with eyes to read and ears to hear:

I will control my tongue, and will not allow it to speak mean, vulgar or profane word.

I will control my thoughts.

I will control my actions.

I will gladly listen to the advice of older and wiser people; I will reverence the wishes of those who love and care for me, and who know life and me better than I. I will develop independence and wisdom to think for myself.

I will try to find out what my duty is as a good American, and my duty I will do, whether it is easy or hard.

I will be honest, in word and in act. I will not lie, sneak, or pretend.

I will be loyal to my family. I will be loyal to my town, my state, my country.

Think of the birth control clinics, the homosexual and feminist lobbies, and the cleansing of high-minded ideals from our children's textbooks and see how far we have fallen in forty-seven years.

In 1941, the *NEA Handbook* spelled out what ought to be expected of teachers hired for the critical purpose of preparing the next generation. Imagine these requirements being made today. The NEA would call a strike. In a section titled "The Future Teachers of America Pledge," there was this:

Physical vitality. I will try to keep my body well and strong.

Mental vigor. I will study daily to keep my mind active and alert.

Moral Discrimination. I will seek to know the right and to live by it.

Wholesome personality. I will cultivate in myself goodwill, friendliness, poise, upright bearing, and careful speech.

Helpfulness. I will learn the art of helping others by doing helpful things daily in school and home.

Knowledge. I will fill my mind with worthy thoughts by observing the beautiful world around me, by reading the best books, and by associating with the best companions.

Leadership. I will make my influence count on the side of right, avoiding habits that weaken and destroy.

These things will I do now that I may be worthy of the high office of teacher.

One wonders why the NEA, which ceased publishing its *Handbook* in 1968, doesn't update and reprint it. The reason is obvious. The NEA and all public higher education is pursuing a different agenda, a different politic, a different citizenship. But the fruits of these pursuits are everywhere, from military people who would betray their country to soul-impoverished college students who regard such NEA concepts as quaint, irrelevant, and the product of Jim Jones-like cultists.

CHILDREN OF LIGHT

The place to begin the ethical overhaul is in our schools. The public schools as constituted are totally lost. Anyone who thinks the public schools can or will provide the answer to the ethical collapse also must believe in the tooth fairy. The public schools are the problem, not the solution.

The Christian school movement is the answer, and church members with children ought to immediately remove them from public schools and put them in Christian schools or, if possible, begin a home schooling program.

Where there are no Christian schools, they should be started. There should be no compromise on the quality of education or the spiritual enrichment. Public education fails when it seeks to divorce the intellectual from a transcendent reference point. Such faulty logic is like keeping a car's engine and transmission separate. The car would never go anywhere.

To those who would argue that our children are "ambassadors" for Christ and, as such, ought to remain in the public schools, I would ask them how many nations send out eight-year-old ambassadors? Soldiers about to be sent into battle are trained first; they understand the weapons of warfare and the behavioral patterns of the enemy before they engage in combat.

The battle over ethics and national direction is being lost because Christians have allowed the secular mind-set of public education to control their children. Young adults with this mental framework will not please their parents or God. Secularism is a lie.

If we want to produce people who share the values of a democratic culture, they must be taught those values and not be left to acquire them by chance.

Chapter Six

Down Come Baby and All

The makers of aspirin are ecstatic over a recent medical report that indicates an aspirin a day may keep heart attacks away and prevent a recurrence in those who have already had one.

Yet when it comes to other maladies, the response from the medical and political elite is a lot less certain.

In Washington, D.C., officials have decided to install a day-care facility in a junior high school just in case people don't use the condoms they are distributing.

Our cultural decline, like the gradual decline of the British Empire, is now certain. Rather than attack the problem, as with aspirin for heart attacks, we seek to manage it.

This is too much even for the liberal intelligentsia, whose constant push for expanding individual rights without individual responsibility caused the decadence that now acts as an undertow, pulling us further and further below the churning waters.

In the 8 February 1988 issue of *The New Republic,* an article titled "The Culture of Apathy," says, "The facts are clear. Licentiousness about drugs and sex have put our children at risk. . . . Lives are ruined by the ethos of 'anything goes.'. . . Is it only conservatives who are to worry about whether wholesomeness will survive the 20th century?"

The New Republic goes as far as to describe what is taking place under our noses as "barbarism": "By barbarism we mean the exacerbated cultural degradation of man and environment."

If this were merely another tome from a right-wing organization, some might dismiss it as predictable stuff. But here we have *The New Republic,* a holy grail to liberals, excoriating the Left for its failure to come to grips with the observable fact that the ship is sinking and we had better either plug the hole or man the lifeboats.

BORN OF THE FLESH

The T. C. Williams High School is located in Alexandria, Virginia, in the wealthy suburbs of Washington, D.C. The school decided to establish a school-based clinic, one of the fastest growing franchises in America.

As with other school districts in the country, a majority of the Alexandria school board and local politicians believe that making birth-control devices available to teenagers, who must still bring a note from home for the school to administer aspirin, will reduce unwanted pregnancies and venereal disease.

The facts prove otherwise. Like those who promised

that legalized gambling would reduce our tax burdens (it hasn't), the proponents of school-based clinics will not be able to reduce pregnancies and sexual diseases. They are buying time because they don't want to face the consequences of a value-free culture.

In an article for *The Washington Post*'s Sunday "Outlook" section on 29 November 1987, Patrick Welsh, a former English teacher at T. C. Williams High School, portrayed the amoral attitudes of many modern teenagers who see nothing at all wrong with having sex and who are oblivious to any man-made or God-made standard. This amorality is worse than immorality. With immorality there is a standard to which one can appeal to bring back the errant. With amorality no one acknowledges the existence of any standard at all.

This indifferent attitude was reflected by a T. C. Williams honors student: "There's a feeling that it's okay for us to have sex because we're educated and know what's going on. We're not going to get pregnant and burden society with unwanted children. We're going to college and have a future. If we do slip up, we'll get an abortion."

These students feel no guilt about what they are doing because they have rewritten the original Author's moral code. "A lot of kids believe in God but just don't think God disapproves of their sex lives," said Will Peyton, a National Merit semi-finalist. If someone were to show Will what the Bible says about sex and its proper place, Will and his friends would say that it doesn't apply to today or that there are different interpretations of what it means.

Patrick Welsh wrote: "The general feeling among scores of middle-class kids I talked to is that as long as high-school couples are 'going together' and are faithful to each other—even if the relationship lasts only a few months—sexual intercourse is fine. Even among those kids who are not sexually active there seems to be an amazingly tolerant and casual attitude towards friends who are."

In addition to deceiving themselves about the consequences of sex too soon, these children, Welsh's article showed, have also become proficient in deceiving their parents. We are asked to condemn the "immorality" of lying in the Iran-Contra scandal but find children's deception of their parents perfectly natural.

Said one teenager to Welsh: "Parents are only around their own kids and their own kids deceive them. I've one friend who has had ten big parties in her house in the last year, and her parents, who've been out of town during each of them, have no idea about it. If they can't even find out about wild parties, how can they be expected to find out about their kids' private sex lives?"

Listen to the hollow and sad voices of other current and former T. C. Williams students.

Jim Dawes, University of Pennsylvania freshman and T. C. Williams valedictorian, 1987: "I could count the number of virgins in my high school peer group on the fingers of both hands. And most of those were on a rampage to lose their virginity during senior year because they thought that being a virgin in college was unacceptable."

Katherine Reilly, T. C. Williams, 1988: "There are a lot more virgins in high school than people think. It's just that virginity isn't the gossipy subject that sex is. Nobody's going to come to school on Monday morning and say, 'Hey, guess what I didn't do Saturday night!' A lot of virgins are afraid to admit it, so people just assume they are sexually active."

Kyra Cook, William and Mary freshman, T. C. Williams, 1987: "In eighth grade, if a couple was sleeping together, it was big news. But it's no big deal in high school. If a couple is dating for a few months, everyone just assumes they're having sex. There's no stigma at all to it. Girls no longer try to hide it. In my class the majority of girls were sleeping with guys but only two or three had 'bad reputations,' and they slept with everyone."

Leyl Master, National Merit semi-finalist, T. C. Williams, 1988: "Teenagers avoid thinking about AIDS because it scares them. I hear girls who are on the pill say if they're going to have sex with a guy a lot that it's not worth the trouble of using a condom every time. A girl who has sex with a guy without a condom a few times simply feels, 'Whatever he's got, I've got,' and just doesn't think about it anymore. They don't like to face the fact that the person they're having sex with could have slept with someone who had AIDS."

Welsh concluded from such comments: "What we may be seeing in the attitudes of these young people is not Sodom and Gomorrah revisited but an attempt to formulate an ethical code that judges sex in terms of individual personal relationships instead of absolute religious and moral codes. The students' ethics condemns promiscuity as degrading, but approves of sex between teenagers committed to each other. Even many teenagers who come from staunch Catholic homes say that the church's strict teaching on premarital sex has little relevance. 'Our parents' beliefs about sex and religion just don't carry over to too many of us. Most kids make their decisions based on their own conscience and on how committed to the other person they are,' says a sixteen-year-old member of a local parish."

Having read these comments from children who could

be yours or mine, doesn't it give you a feeling of empti-
ness? Life is a great teacher, and these children who feel
no guilt and no remorse for what they are doing now will
feel it someday. They have only to ask their own parents
how they feel now if they adopted the sixties attitude
of free love. In fact, the chickens have come home to
roost for the love children of the sixties. They trashed
their own parents' ethics and now are receiving interest
on their own ethical investment—wayward children and
broken hearts.

The school-based health clinics that are trumpeted as
the solution to unwanted pregnancies and venereal diseases have already proved miserable failures even as they
are being promoted as the answer to the problem.

Writing in the 14 October 1986 edition of *The Wall
Street Journal*, Stan E. Weed, director of the independent
Institute for Research and Evaluation in Salt Lake City,
said: "As the number and proportion of teenage family-
planning clients increased, we observed a corresponding
increase in the teenage pregnancy and abortion rates:
50 to 120 more pregnancies per thousand clients, rather
than the 200 to 300 fewer pregnancies as estimated by
researchers at the Alan Guttmacher Institute (formerly
the research arm of the Planned Parenthood Federation). We find that greater teenage participation in such
clinics led to lower teen birthrates. However, the impact
on the abortion and total pregnancy rates was exactly
opposite the stated intentions of the program. The original problems appear to have grown worse."

BORN OF THE SPIRIT

It is not just a question of our children developing their
"own" ethic or of the sex merchants making false claims

about reducing the consequences of illicit sex. The real issue is that the only ethic for building stable and whole lives has been ignored. That's why we are in such deep trouble. Only a return to that singular ethic will produce the results we say we want but which we have demonstrated we cannot get in any other way.

When I was a child, a Washington, D.C., bread company used an advertising slogan: "Helps build strong bodies twelve ways."

What is needed in America is a return to the only ethic that has ever built strong bodies, minds, and spirits. It is time to stop apologizing for it or being intimidated by the so-called civil libertarians who have been largely responsible for tearing down this ethic and contributing to the ethical chaos that now confronts us.

Writing in the book *School-Based Clinics,* Bryce J. Christensen, editor of *Family America,* quoted the president of the Rockford Institute, John Howard, who has observed that "recent calls for 'excellence' in academic performance would not solve the problems of the American schools until 'lawfulness, civility, morality, ethics . . . and a deference to mature and informed judgment' were restored to their proper priority. As long ago as 1958, Dorothy Thompson complained in *Ladies' Home Journal* that public school teachers no longer 'recognized the value of character building' and that many were positively undermining character in children. Speaking in 1985 to the National Press Club in Washington, D.C., Brigham Young University President Jeffrey Holland observed that the idea that 'the school should . . . be able to take a stand on what is ethically sound' has become 'a notion at risk in the 1980s.'

"Nor is the problem confined to the high schools and grade schools. The respected intellectual historian James

Billington, director of the Woodrow Wilson International Center for Scholars, told *U.S. News & World Report* in 1984 that 'American universities have fallen down on the job of transmitting values to students. There has been a tendency to create courses of study that contain no values whatever.' Steven Muller, president of Johns Hopkins University, conceded in 1980 that 'the biggest failing in higher education today is that we fall short in exposing students to values. Our failure . . . means that universities are turning out potentially highly skilled barbarians.'"

Something John Stott, the English clergyman, told me in the early 1970s has stuck in my mind. Stott said the principles of the Bible work whether or not one acknowledges their source. It seems to me that a unified moral ethic based on biblical principles is the only one that has a proven track record.

With this ethic in mind, the questions that need to be asked are: "what kind of people do we want to be and how do we wish to be remembered by history?" The answers to these questions ought to determine our legal, moral, and medical strategy. They will also determine our future as a nation.

As psychologist James Dobson has written, "Permissiveness has not just been a failure; it's been a disaster."

It's time for some disaster relief.

Part Three

Preserving Domestic Tolerability

Chapter Seven

To Thine Own Self Be True

Ethical standards, which once were tied in principle, if not always in practice, to the Golden Rule and to other guidelines emanating from the Old and New Testaments, have not suddenly collapsed. They have been in decline in Europe and America at least since the rise of the Enlightenment in the eighteenth century.

Although religious revivals sometimes slowed creeping secularization for as long as a generation, the general downward spiral of standards has continued because people have not actively implemented the teachings of Christ and his Gospel in their lives. Now, a plurality, if not a majority, build their lives on a foundation of self-interest and moral relativism. This reasoning finds its expression in the often-heard liberal view: "If you want to pray in private, that's fine and no one is stopping you, but don't try to bring your religious ideas into the marketplace." This is nothing more than a form of spiritual apartheid.

THE UNKINDEST CUT OF ALL

The conscience of Christianity has been cut out, and no one seems to care. Sadly, even many who say they are Bible-believing Christians have taken up the liberal litany and, in so doing, participate in the de-Christianization of the culture.

Although de-Christianization and declericalization are both aspects of the secularization process that has been at work in the Western world for several centuries, they must be distinguished carefully. Declericalization has been basically a positive trend, seeking to free society from the control or manipulation of churches and clergy. It involves the legitimate separation of church and state, recognizing that the church is a voluntary association with spiritual goals and that the state's task is to promulgate public justice for the entire citizenry. De-Christianization, on the other hand, is harmful because it undermines the public character of authority and morality as rooted in Scripture and Western tradition and replaces them with relativistic and pragmatic values that range from irresponsible individualism to arbitrary authoritarianism. Our concern here is with the harmful effects of secularization as de-Christianization.

A consistent ethical system cannot be established without an absolute authority as part of one's world-view. An individual's rights, in the absence of such an absolute, are protected only insofar as a majority that believes in those rights remains in power. Should a despot come to power, however, those rights can evaporate overnight. This is precisely what occurred in the French Revolution, and it is why our own revolution was superior because it guaranteed rights based on their endowment from an infinite personal God. This endowment made those rights inalienable, placing them outside the reach of fallen humans.

A caller to a Cable News Network program asserted to me, "I am an agnostic. Why should I care about what the Bible says?" I answered him and all agnostics by noting that biblical principles in the fabric of our culture have allowed the American agnostic freedom of expression. This is in contrast to repression of the Christian or Jew in the Soviet Union where the state has replaced God.

Historically, Christian moral standards have formed the basis of Western society, whether individual leaders were personally Christian or not. These included truthfulness, rightness, and honesty as a basis for moral obligation and for common good.

Modern secular humanism, which makes humanity the center and measure of all things, flowed from the Enlightenment and the French Revolution and brought new attitudes of absolute individualism, pragmatism, moral relativism, and the seeking of personal success. Such attitudes have led to a denial of absolute moral standards. What is "socially good" and acceptable is now determined by majority opinion.

The central attitude of modern secular humanism is personal preference as the highest norm. As Dr. Francis Schaeffer put it, the culture now pursues only two objectives: that of personal peace, by which is meant "You have your life to live, I have mine. You leave me alone and I'll leave you alone" and affluence, by which is meant the pursuit and acquisition of more and more material things.

TRUE DEMOCRACY

Contrary to modern suppositions, "pluralism" does not mean that all positions must be afforded equal weight and equal value. Pluralism simply means that all positions deserve to be fairly heard. Democracy then requires that a choice must be made, often among competing views and values, as to which will ensure the provision for the common defense, promotion of the general welfare, and preservation of domestic tranquility.

In 1829, a French Roman Catholic priest, Felicite Lamennais, became one of the first major thinkers in the Christian tradition to advocate a critical acceptance of democracy. Until then, there were those who were willing to accept the notion of democracy, but on a humanistic, self-directed basis, without Christian underpinnings. Lamennais said that would not work and called for Christian values to permeate the democratic experience.

Prior to Lamennais, most Protestants and Catholics were theocrats who presided over swings of the pendulum from radical individualism to collectivistic despotism and reigns of terror. The French Revolution was a triumph of this latter ideology. A parliamentary majority determined that opponents of the regime should be executed and thousands went to the guillotine. Anticlericalism was also a dominant theme of the revolution.

Lamennais, who lived through this period, saw that democracy could not flourish apart from Christian values. This did not mean then, nor does it mean now, that everyone must personally be a Christian. What it does mean is that if there is no standard higher than the minds of men, then all men are at the mercy of whatever authoritarian elite is able to rise to power. Without Christian values, democracy degenerates into the whim of the majority or the whim of the dictator.

As Lamennais wrote in 1817: "A notion of law is intimately tied to a notion of authority. Every doctrine that destroys a notion of authority likewise demolishes the notion of law."[1] Without God, noted Lamennais, society can be constituted only by the artificial authority of the special interests or the passions of the moment.

Because of the lack of an ultimate authority, politicians must pay homage to humanistic philosophy if they hope to win the approval of voters.

COMMON BLESSING

Although Lamennais strongly influenced many throughout Europe to infuse biblical principles into government structures, the man who was most successful at this task would arrive later in the century. He was a Dutch Protestant named Abraham Kuyper.

Kuyper, who was first a journalist and later a politician, was foremost a thinking Christian who saw no conflict between church and state; in fact, he viewed biblical principles as a guarantee that the work of the state would serve the best interests of churched and unchurched citizens alike.

To those who would suggest today that agnostics and atheists feel threatened by such notions, one need only point out that an agnostic in America, where there is a memory of biblical traditions and thought, is more free than a Christian or Jew in the Soviet Union, where the state is god and all other forms of worship are considered "anti-Soviet."

Kuyper recognized early on that the emancipation of

the common people, 90 percent of whom were denied the right to vote because of a class society, was central to a just and healthy society. The elite in the Netherlands of the mid-1800s were largely property-owning males over the age of thirty, whose world-view did not include much outside of themselves.

While still a young man, Kuyper developed a political strategy not only to emancipate his fellow evangelicals, but also Roman Catholics, socialists, and others who held to political and even religious views different from his own.

Kuyper's efforts were truly pluralistic in nature, but he had a basis for his pluralism: that God offered a common blessing to all and, therefore, within such a context, all should respond by offering an equal opportunity for everyone to fully participate in the life of a society. Kuyper's position did not flow from some sentimental, humanistic feeling designed to win him votes and deliver him to power. He understood himself as the servant of God and the state as an instrument of God to be used to establish justice.

Kuyper's two main instruments in forging a true pluralization of his society were his newspaper, *The Standard,* of which he was the editor for many years, and his Christian political party, the Anti-Revolutionary party.

In Kuyper's life and in his newspaper he presumed a standard of truth unlike contemporary publications that seem to be on a constant search for meaning even while they deny in their editorials that truth exists. They focus on the sensational, the bizarre, and the attempts to find solutions through the political process alone.

Most of Kuyper's editorials had a few simple points that cumulatively provided readers with an education in politics and world-views. The sheer volume of these editorials on many topics was, in itself, impressive.

Kuyper skillfully used repetition and rhetorical questions such as "Do you favor sin, revolution, liberalism, secular humanism? If not, follow me to receive the truth."

In contrast, today's pollsters seek information rather than truth. As a result, opinions rather than verities guide our nation.

Imagine an American political leader saying what Kuyper once said: "The other parties campaign for parliamentary seats, more or less; we campaign for our principles!" Kuyper was able to say that he never lost an election because the publicizing of his principles was always a victory in itself.

Today neither sin nor principles are debated. Because there are no standards or values, principled people are usually considered intolerant.

Kuyper ran national political campaigns every two years between 1873 and 1917, getting people elected to Parliament and, ultimately, getting himself elected as prime minister in 1901.

The current prime minister of the Netherlands, Ruud Lubbers, noted Kuyper's contribution to the vitality of his nation on the occasion of the one hundred fiftieth anniversary of Kuyper's birth.

Lubbers said that Kuyper had made two contributions of lasting significance to national politics. One was the realization that the social issue of poverty was not simply a question of mercy, but of the state's God-given task of promoting public justice. The second was Kuyper's emphasis on the creation of a truly pluralistic society in which different philosophical communities meet their social responsibilities through separate institutions.

At a memorial service in Maassluis, evangelical

historian George Puchinger praised Kuyper for his insight into the reality of the origins and development of spiritual diversity in the Dutch nation.

He said Kuyper demonstrated brilliantly that the "public character of religion" must have its place even in a neutral state.

As Kuyper believed, the notion of true pluralism only works effectively when Christian values are dominant in a culture. For it is only the biblical values that ascribe and impart the highest view and value to human beings. Apart from these views and values, anyone can be manipulated and used for the pleasure and purpose of whoever is able to muster the most arms or votes. No one has intrinsic value.

To those who say such a view imposes one set of values on others and that this is against the traditions of our own nation, it is important to realize that someone's values must always be supreme. It is not accurate to say that "neutral values," as if there was any such thing, are to be preferred over Christian values.

Kuyper addressed this objection in a 8 January 1874 editorial in his newspaper: "Equal rights for all! We give freedom to the Jew, Catholic, liberal or conservative, who does not acknowledge God's Word in politics, provided they also grant us our freedom. Therefore we call for a widening of the vote. Conviction must be measured against conviction."

The point, I think, is that for both politics and life to have meaning, one must have a reference point. Although Kuyper was willing to offer total freedom to those who would disagree with his religious presuppositions (and could do so because that freedom is also granted by God), he said that for the purpose of "promoting the general welfare" his own reference point would be God and his Word. In so doing, Kuyper provided a separation between church and state while preserving the original relationships of God, humanity, and government. He recognized that God had given two different sets of instructions, one for the church and the other for the state. The task for the church is to preach the gospel and exercise spiritual discipline, while the task for the state is to promulgate public justice for all.

DOING THE TRUTH

As church history professor Martin Marty wrote in a 20 December 1987 edition of *The Los Angeles Times,* "The ancient Hebrews and the authors of the Greek New Testament spoke little about truth in the abstract, about truth in the impersonal sense. Instead they connected 'truth' with the character of a faithful God and then wanted to see that quality reflected in humans.

"The biblical concept richer than 'telling the truth' is expressed as 'doing the truth.' When someone 'does' the truth, we can check that person out more readily than when talk about truth is only an intellectual game or tease.

"'Doing the Truth' relied on the Hebrew concept of *emeth,* connoting faithfulness and reliability. It moves from the deepest claims about the character of God to the richest images in the humans who mirror that character. It also works among those unmoved by explicit faith in God but still living as people on whom we can count. The truth is 'in' them and they 'are' truth because they 'do' truth. We say they have integrity.

"The test of such truth is obvious. Say, 'she's as good as her word' or 'his handshake is better than a contract' and you describe someone who embodies what today's truth seekers are looking for."

PUBLIC AFFECTIONS

Marty concluded: "The role of leadership in cultures that nurture honesty is crucial, but the search for such a culture is complicated when a free media effectively exposes liars among leaders. So it is important to develop other places to look alongside public leadership.

"I suggest what eighteenth-century British statesman Edmund Burke spoke of as a need to develop 'public affections,' the positive connections where trust and loyalty emerge. Burke argued that 'we begin our public affections in our families.' Then we move out to 'our neighborhoods and our habitual provincial connection. These are inns and resting places' along the way to what he called 'the great country in which the heart found something which it could build.'

"Burke connected with the 'affections' what I now connect with trust and truth. 'To be attached to the subdivision, to love the little platoon we belong to in society, is the first principle . . . of public affections. It is the first link in the series by which we proceed towards a love to our country and to mankind.' Then people must learn to 'do' the truth in the family again, where the stakes are highest and the tests more available; if then they move through friendship and neighborhood, through college and church and club and cause, in circles where someone stands up for truth and many learn to do it, the 'first principle' of public truth telling would begin to emerge. America could be a country putting a new premium on truth."

Marty then makes a central point from which lessons

can be drawn and applied in the case of the Wall Street and television religion scandals as well as the crisis in politics and government leadership: "The liars and deceivers of recent exposure were so often loners, celebrities who had admirers and groupies but not friends who could be critical, who could keep them honest.

"The public responds with 'the character issue.' Character requires context. The French novelist Stendhal wrote that 'One can acquire anything in solitude except character,' and Goethe proposed that 'Character calls forth character.' The right company can help us in our little platoons to develop a culture where people aspire to truth, still 'the fundamental requirement of human life.'"

THE STEADY DRUMBEAT

A basic fact of the nineteenth century was that the idea of neutral politics and a neutral view of life were gaining ground. Kuyper had read Lamennais, and he was also aware that the greatest threat to Christianity and the values that sprang from it was not outright atheism but indifference.

Kuyper saw the approaching crisis for believers. Yet because he saw that both sin and grace are operative in history, he avoided a totally negative and pessimistic approach. The problem of modernity is a historical fact that the believer must seek to understand with a positive attitude.

The Bible, Kuyper believed, is relevant not only for personal matters, but also should serve as a guide for public matters as well. Thus the standard of God's Word must be raised in society. The name of Kuyper's daily newspaper, *The Standard*, emphasized this conviction about the universal relevance of Scripture.

The Bible, Kuyper emphasized, contains the first principles concerning human nature, life's purpose, and the state's task. Although the church should have the exclusive responsibility of speaking about sin and salvation, the Scriptures clearly outline the state's task of promoting the common good. To ignore these teachings or to declare them irrelevant sets humanity on a course that will be forever unfulfilling. It would be like discovering that holy water cures cancer but having a court rule that the cure is invalid on First Amendment grounds and ordering medical researchers to seek nonreligiously based cures.

The Christian who understands that the world is fallen and that sin's impact infects and affects everything we do recognizes that this is an abnormal world.

But the unbeliever sees what surrounds him as normal and tries to bring order, perfection, and hope out of a situation that, from the Christian perspective, is abnormal, imperfect, and hopeless apart from God.

These two radically different world-views inevitably lead to different policies and different conclusions. If one person believes that God has a role to play in his life and nation, he is more likely to think and act far differently in that life and as a citizen than the one who believes, as Carl Sagan does, that "the cosmos is all there has been."

In the program for his Anti-Revolutionary party, adopted in 1879, Kuyper spelled out five principles for political action. Among them was his view that the source of sovereign authority for the state is to be found in God and not in popular sovereignty or majority vote.

This view is not theocratic in that it seeks to persuade rather than dictate. Kuyper believed that if culture affirmed biblical principles in educational institutions, in political parties, and in the media, there would be a steady drumbeat that would compel people to march to his drummer.

Today there is a drumbeat, but it is in favor of views and values that are the antithesis of what Kuyper espoused. It is the drumbeat of secular humanism and hedonism.

Kuyper's goal was to build a public presence for Christian norms based upon an appeal to conscience and to use the resulting change in people's convictions as a basis for promoting biblical principles through the democratic process.

The phrase "separation of church and state" does not appear in the Constitution, but it has been used to separate Christians from culture. This was a philosophy totally foreign to Abraham Kuyper and to our founding fathers. It is also not the teaching of the Bible. We have created a modern system of catacombs with underground Christians preaching to themselves and maintaining a separate culture. This philosophy of separation has not brought positive changes to our culture.[2]

Chapter Eight

Nothing But the Truth

Good family life is a nation's most precious asset. It is the seed of values, and people with values are the mighty oaks of a free land. If America loses its families, its values, and its freedoms, we can only blame ourselves for doing too little, too late.

FIRST FAMILY

Reporter Ray Richard told the sad story of a family gone awry in the 17 December 1987 edition of the *Boston Globe:* "The long-distance call came on Thanksgiving Day, as Jerry and his four young children ate turkey at the home of a friend.

"'I'm not coming back,' the caller said. 'You can keep the kids.'

"The caller was Jerry's wife, the mother of the children, two of them not yet in school."

127

The story goes on to tell how the wife, upon learning of her husband's diagnosis of cancer, decided she never expected to be forced to live up to the "in sickness and in health" part of the marriage vow and left town. Jerry is now on welfare as he battles his disease. He appealed for help through the newspaper's hardship fund so that his children might at least have some toys and clothing for Christmas.

The "civil libertarians," who would protect pornographers rather than their victims, and the feminists, who have worked diligently to undermine the commitment that has held families together, have sown a terrible and long-lasting wind. Now, people like Jerry and his children (and their children who may also suffer) are reaping the undeserved whirlwind.

Is love really never having to say you're sorry? Self-love, perhaps, but not real love.

The ethical dilemma we face can be compared to a stream of pure water, which, after years of having toxic substances dumped into it, is no longer fit for swimming or drinking. The fish have died, and the stream smells so bad that people avoid it.

Feminist Insanity

The ethical breakdown can be said to have been fostered and/or fueled by the destruction of the family, and the crisis in the family can in large part be placed at the door of the so-called women's liberation movement, which ought to be more accurately described as the "women's bondage movement."

Feminism has not liberated women or men. Instead it has contributed to the dissolution of family ties and blurred role models that have been a singular source of strength for this nation and for the advancement of Western culture for centuries. The family was not created because social scientists thought it was a good way to deliver the mail. The family was ordained by God for the benefit of man and as a microcosm of the relationship in the Trinity.

But we have consistently sought to put asunder that which God has joined together. The resulting chaos has produced a record of social decay and decline perhaps unmatched in the history of this country.

Even some major denominations, rather than stand for truth, have sought to accommodate the spirit of the age, believing that popularity is more important than doctrine and proper orthodoxy. In recent years, Lutherans, United Methodists, Episcopalians, and some Presbyterians have joined the United Church of Christ and Unitarian Universalists in creating divorce prayers and even divorce ceremonies, featuring family and invited guests to "undo" marriages.

In the Unitarian ceremony, the couple is given the chance to recite words of respect and lay aside bitterness through responsive readings led by a so-called minister. Marriage vows are repealed, and the couple hand their wedding rings to the minister.

The Unitarian service ends with a pronouncement from the minister that the marriage is dissolved, and the couple is supposed to shake hands.

Unfortunately, for the guests who attended the wedding there is no provision in this service for the return of the wedding gifts.

The conservative Jewish writer Norman Podhoretz criticized the twenty-five years of feminist "contributions" to American life in a 21 August 1987 column in *The Washington Post.* Podhoretz began by asking the right questions, which have more to do with results than with philosophy. He asked whether feminism has a good or bad record and, most importantly, whether women, children, and men are really better off now than before the women's liberation movement burst on the scene in the 1960s, punctuated by the public burning of brassieres.

Wrote Podhoretz: "Women's lib has swept over the past two decades like a tornado, leaving behind it a vast wreckage of broken and twisted lives." He said feminism has helped to produce "broken marriages leading to other broken marriages or to desperate little affairs; children sacrificed to the 'needs' of their parents; women driven literally crazy by bitterness and self-pity while being encouraged to see virtue and health in the indulgence of such feelings; men emasculated by guilt and female bullying all in the name of and for the sake of a new and supposedly superior type of relation between the sexes."

Podhoretz correctly concluded that feminism has exacerbated rather than mitigated female grievances. Even more important, it has made men less rather than more willing to assume responsibility for the women they sleep with and the children they sire, and this lack of responsibility has become perhaps the major complaint of many women today.

The Census Bureau gives weight to this argument. They report that of the 8.8 million women in the United States with children under twenty-one whose fathers were not living at home, only 2.1 million received full child-support payments from the absent father.

The rest of the mothers, according to the survey of 1985 data, lacked a court order for child support, or, despite having one, received no money or less than the stipulated amount.

Payments for those women receiving child support averaged $2,220 annually—down from $2,350 in 1983 even with adjustments for inflation.

Why should men feel a responsibility to support their children and to remain with their wives when feminism and the entire culture have preached for twenty-five years that the only responsibility we should feel is to ourselves and that even marriage can be an experience akin to incarceration.

The Census Bureau report also looked at alimony payments, finding that the average payment is only $3,733 a year. That means the woman must either work or accept welfare. Profound social consequences flow from either of these dead ends.

It is true that the sins of the father (and mother) will be visited on the children. Norman Podhoretz said that the sins of feminism have produced a "deep and disabling confusion about what as males and females they really want and need from each other."

This is progress? This is liberation? This is regress, bondage, and self-destruction, but few are willing to speak against it because the so-called leaders in government, media, and education fear criticism for getting off the humanistic merry-go-round. They say and do nothing; and, like an untreated infection, the problem worsens.

Family Integrity

What does integrity mean for the family? Despite recent surveys that show a slight drop in the divorce rate, we continue to experience the highest number of divorces of any free and civilized nation in history. The Census Bureau reported in 1985 that 60 percent of post-Baby Boom women in their thirties can expect to be divorced. The national average for everyone else is about 50 percent.

Think of the sociological and psychological fallout on millions of children from these broken marriages. It will trickle down to the third and fourth generations.

Former Massachusetts Democratic Senator Paul Tsongas wrote a book in 1983 called *Heading Home.* It told of his struggle with cancer and his decision to leave the Senate for the sake of his family. Some people plan, work, dream, and spend huge amounts of money to win a seat in the U.S. Senate, but Tsongas found strength and affirmation in what may seem to some to be the strangest of places.

"I felt totally alien," wrote Tsongas. "I was one of the select few in the United States Senate—the most exclusive club in the world. I did not want membership in a club of the afflicted. . . . [I] began the rapid descent into despair. What was there to fight for? What was there to hope for? What was there to pray for?"

Then, in one of the book's most poignant moments, Tsongas, who eschewed the party-and-dinner circuit in Washington so that he could devote more time to his wife and three daughters, allows us to identify with him at a deep level: "I was no longer the Senator from Massachusetts. I was a frightened human being who loved his wife and children, and desperately wanted to live."

The book is packed with one of the least sought after and least appreciated character qualities in Washington or anywhere else—humility.

If Tsongas were to write his own epitaph, he could not have said it better than when he tells his wife, Niki, "You know, after ten years in this town, all that I will be remembered for is the fact that I loved my wife."

"And what's wrong with that?" Niki replies.
What's wrong, indeed? That's integrity in family life.

MORE VALUE

In a remarkable commencement address to graduating seniors at Duke University on Sunday, 10 May 1987, ABC anchorman Ted Koppel sounded like one of those right-wing, fundamentalist ministers the press so often derides. He selected ethics and morals as his main theme to these children of the sexual revolution!

In his deadly serious address, Koppel deplored the superficiality of a culture that elevates a Vanna White to stardom on television's "Wheel of Fortune."

Condemning the media's hedonistic messages, Koppel harkened back to his parents' generation and told the Duke students, "We have actually convinced ourselves that slogans will save us. 'Shoot up if you must, but use a clean needle.' 'Enjoy sex whenever and with whomever you wish, but wear a condom.'"

Then in what must have seemed like a lecture from their parents (do parents still give such lectures or have they given up?), Koppel said: "No. The answer is no. Not no because it isn't cool . . . or smart . . . or because you might end up in jail or dying in an AIDS ward—but no . . . because it's wrong. Because we have spent five thousand years as a race of rational human beings trying to drag ourselves out of the primeval slime by searching for truth . . . and moral absolutes."

Moral absolutes? I checked quickly to make sure I was not reading a sermon by a television evangelist. No it was Koppel, who continued: "In the place of Truth [his capitalization] we have discovered facts; for moral absolutes we have substituted moral ambiguity. We now communicate with everyone . . . and say absolutely nothing. We have reconstructed the Tower of Babel and it is a television antenna. A thousand voices producing a daily parody of democracy; in which everyone's opinion is afforded equal weight; regardless of substance or merit. Indeed, it can even be argued that opinions of real weight tend to sink with barely a trace in television's ocean of banalities.

"Our society finds Truth too strong a medicine to digest undiluted. In its purest form Truth is not a polite tap on the shoulder; it is a howling reproach.

"What Moses brought down from Mount Sinai were not the Ten Suggestions . . . they are Commandments. *Are,* not were."

What is even more amazing than Ted Koppel delivering a commencement address like this at a major American university in the 1980s is that the students were willing to listen to it.

Koppel continued: "The sheer brilliance of the Ten Commandments is that they codify, in a handful of words, acceptable human behavior. Not just for then . . . or now . . . but for all time. Language evolves . . . power shifts from nation to nation. . . . Man erases one frontier after another; and yet we and our behavior . . . and the Commandments which govern that behavior . . . remain the same.

"The tension between those Commandments and our baser instincts provides the grist for journalism's daily mill. What a huge, gaping void there would be in our informational flow and in our entertainment without the routine violation of the Sixth Commandment. Thou shalt not murder.

"On what did the Hart campaign founder? On accusations that he violated the Seventh Commandment: Thou shalt not commit adultery. Relevant? Of course the Commandments are relevant. Simply because we use different terms and tools, the Eighth Commandment is still relevant to the insider trading scandal. The Commandments don't get bogged down in methodology. Simple and to the point. Thou shalt not steal. Watch the Iran-Contra hearings and keep the Ninth Commandment in mind: Thou shalt not bear false witness. And the Tenth Commandment, which seems to have been crafted for the 80s and the 'Me' generation. The Commandment against covetous desires; against longing for anything we cannot get in an honest and legal fashion.

"When you think about it, it's curious, isn't it? We've changed in almost all things—where we live, how we eat, communicate, travel; and yet, in our moral and immoral behavior we are fundamentally unchanged.

"Maimonedes and Jesus summed it up in almost identical words: 'Thou shalt love thy neighbor as thyself. Do unto others as you would have them do unto you.' So much for our obligations toward our fellowmen. That's what the last five Commandments are all about.

"The first five are more complex in that they deal with figures of moral authority. The Fifth Commandment requires us to honor our father and mother. Religious scholars through the years have concluded that it was inscribed on the first tablet . . . among the laws and piety toward God because, as far as their children are concerned, parents stand in the place of God. What a strange conclusion! Us in the place of God. We, who set such flawed examples for you."

Koppel then concluded with some remarkable insights for a man who is not viewed as part of a religious community.

Koppel said the First Commandment was the "most

controversial of the Commandments" because it "requires that we believe in the existence of a single supreme God. And then, in the Second, Third and Fourth Commandments, *prohibits* the worship of any other gods, *forbids* that his name be taken in vain, *requires* that we set aside one day in seven to rest and worship Him" [emphasis his].

Then, in perhaps the most poignant moment, Koppel sounded like a preacher reaching the conclusion of his sermon: "I caution you, as one who performs daily on that flickering altar, to set your sights beyond what you can see. There is true majesty in the concept of an unseen power which can neither be measured nor weighed. There is harmony and inner peace to be found in following a moral compass that points in the same direction, regardless of fashion or trend."

The supreme irony of the speech is that Koppel delivered it to an audience of students, most of whom are from public schools in which even the posting of the Ten Commandments has been forbidden by federal courts as an unconstitutional act. Such rulings have elevated a misguided interpretation of the First Amendment to a position of greater power and worship than the First Commandment. Indeed, in our contemporary world, the courts have decreed "thou shalt have no other gods before the state."

A better illustration of C. S. Lewis's complaint could not be found. Lewis observed that we have made "men without chests. We have removed the organ, but demand the function."

Moral Flabbiness

Allan Bloom has said: "The moral education that is today supposed to be the great responsibility of the family cannot exist if it cannot present to the imagination of the young a vision of a moral cosmos and of the rewards and punishments for good and evil, sublime speeches that accompany and interpret deeds, protagonists and antagonists in the drama of moral choice, a sense of the stakes involved in such choice, and the despair that results when the world is 'disenchanted'. Otherwise, education becomes the vain attempt to give children 'values'."

Bloom pointed out that parents are not prepared to help their children. "Beyond the fact that parents do not know what they believe, and surely do not have the self-confidence to tell their children much more than that they want them to be happy and fulfill whatever potential they may have, values are such pallid things. What are they and how are they communicated?"[1]

Schools are not equipped to provide training. "The courses in 'values clarification' springing up in the schools are supposed to provide models for parents and get children to talk about abortion, sexism and the arms race, issues the significance of which they cannot possibly understand. Such education is little more than propaganda, and propaganda that does not work, because the opinions of values arrived at are will-o'-the-wisps, insubstantial, without ground in reasoning. Such 'values' will inevitably change as public opinion changes. The new moral education has none of the genius that engenders moral instinct or second nature, the prerequisite not only of character but also of thought."

Bloom noted that families in the end provide little moral education. "Actually, the family's moral training now comes down to inculcating the bare minima of social behavior, not lying or stealing, and produces university students who can say nothing more about the ground of their moral action than 'if I did that to him, he could do it to me'—an explanation which does not even satisfy those who utter it."[2]

We have become a nation dedicated to the perfect body. Commercials on television and advertisements in newspapers compel us to work out on Nautilus machines. Joggers line the highways at six o'clock in the morning. High-fiber diets promise us protection from colon cancer.

But what about the spiritual dimension of life—the one that produces the character traits we say we really admire in men and women? Have we succeeded as a nation when we have developed perfect bodies but have left the soul undernourished and undeveloped? Sadly, today's students do not even know anything about soul development.

Bloom said he often asked his students, "Who do you think is evil?" Most responded by saying, "Hitler." Rarely do students mention Stalin any longer. There are no other answers. A few years ago some might have mentioned Nixon, but he has been rehabilitated by *Newsweek* and by himself. That's it. There is no concept of evil, much less the identification of anyone who *is* evil.

In fact, following President Reagan's speech in Orlando, Florida, to the National Association of Evangelicals in which he referred to the Soviet Union as an "evil empire," Anthony Lewis of *The New York Times* wrote a column debunking the very concept of evil and suggesting that it doesn't exist. Just give everyone a B. F. Skinner behavior modification course and the world will be all right, Lewis seemed to be suggesting.

When I say moral and spiritual development, I don't mean just the knowledge and study of the Bible, our best-selling book, though that is an excellent starting point. It has been the starting point for some of our greatest leaders, Lincoln among them. I also mean the great thinkers of the past and at least a nodding acquaintance with good music, art, poetry, and literature. How will our children know what great writing, art, and music are unless they are exposed to it? Sadly, what passes for education today in some quarters is the equivalent of intellectual junk food. We have failed to teach our sons and daughters to think critically.

I have spoken on more than seventy college campuses. I have found most students appallingly retarded in their ability to think critically, even at Harvard. One student told me it was unnecessary to have a set of fixed absolutes in order to arrive at an enduring moral and political order. I said, "Assuming that you are not an anarchist, on what would you found a society?" The student responded, "My socialization process."

I said, "What if my socialization process differs from yours?"

She said, "Then I would just have to get people who agree with me together to fight you and those who agree with you."

"Congratulations," I said. "You have just made the case for Adolph Hitler, Joseph Stalin, and every other tyrant in the world who believes that might makes right."

There is a window of opportunity for those who have had enough and wish to regain control of the direction of our country. Even Norman Lear, who founded the misnamed "People for the American Way," recently said, "For all of our alarm, it is clear that the religious right is responding to a real hunger in our society . . . a deep-seated yearning for stable values." I read this quote in *The Washington Post* so I know it is true!

Tom Hayden, the radical activist of the sixties and husband of Jane Fonda, attended his thirtieth high school reunion in Michigan and said of his generation: "We started by believing that we were masters of our own destinies. That's what knitted us together. We learned we couldn't control our own lives. Our marriages broke up. We were sure of the contours and stability of our nation, and then a president was shot. We wanted civil rights and poverty put at the top of the agenda, and we got the Vietnam War."

Moral Forces

In Bristol, Virginia, on the Tennessee border, teachers are taking another look at and using the nineteenth-century *McGuffey Eclectic Readers* because they emphasize the virtues of patriotism and the work ethic. School officials say the books will give students "something to hold onto other than *E.T.*"

Stories and poems in the *Readers* emphasize honesty, fairness, and punctuality, and they are being used as supplementary material because modern texts lack such values.

At the Edward H. Fitler Elementary School, an old building of dirty granite in working-class Philadelphia, teachers insist that boys and girls form orderly, separate lines when entering or leaving class. "Sure it's old-fashioned and sexist," says school principal William Crumley, Jr., who is forty-seven, "but our parents did it and we do it." In fact, teachers, parents, and pupils are trying to turn back the educational clock at Fitler with strict student dress codes, tough grading, and plenty of attention to individual students. One result: though Fitler is an urban public school with 35 percent white students, 45 percent black, the rest Hispanic and Asian, it boasts a multiracial waiting list of two thousand.

Parents from all over Philadelphia want to send their children there, even though it would mean busing.

For too long, schools have been used by special interest groups to propagandize students instead of educate them. Children ought to be taught that which will perpetuate a society that promotes the general welfare, provides for the common defense, and insures domestic tranquility.

Drugs, teen pregnancy, AIDS, and the rest are the consequences of a value-free society; we cannot end these social blights unless we realize that these are the direct result of what we have been teaching our children. Mandating AIDS education courses from early elementary school through the twelfth grade, as the New York State Board of Regents has done, will not stop AIDS. People still smoke themselves to death despite massive antismoking campaigns and package warnings.

We must diagnose our ailment before treatments are prescribed. Unfortunately, social engineers and timid politicians are force-feeding the medicine before the diagnosis has been properly made.

We are where we are as a nation because we have abandoned where we used to be. And so we must begin with this acknowledgment. Men and women who are not afraid to tell the truth must be encouraged to take the lead in our country and say what needs to be said, unafraid of the criticism and name calling from those who seek legitimacy for their immoral lifestyles.

I liked what Pope John Paul II said to reporters aboard his plane on the way to the United States. Asked about opposition from the liberal Catholic community to his stand on marriage, divorce, abortion, and other issues, the pope responded that he is used to criticism and, besides, he is not the first to be so criticized. The first, he said, was Jesus Christ! One does not have to be Catholic to admire the pope's firm stand.

If we look at the churches in America that are growing and meeting the needs of their people, we find that these churches are almost exclusively within the Evangelical-Fundamentalist framework.

If our nation returns to the basic truths that launched our revolution, undergirded our Constitution, and sustained our country through war, economic upheaval, and other uncertainties, we can prosper again. But if we continue down the path of these last twenty-five years, we will be a footnote in the history books of the tyrants who will occupy this land.

FREEDOM'S HOLY LIGHT

When Pope John Paul II visited the United States in September 1987, he took note of the bicentennial of the U.S. Constitution. While we celebrated the freedom the Constitution has given us, the pope introduced a sober note into the observance. I wrote a newspaper column about it:

"Ten score years ago, our forefathers ratified a Constitution for the newly independent United States of America. In 1787, freedom not only had a purpose and a meaning, it also had a price.

"The freedom our founders sought was not a means for pursuing self-indulgence, but a tool that could, as stated in the Preamble to the Constitution, 'ensure domestic Tranquility, promote the general Welfare, and secure the Blessings of Liberty to ourselves and our Posterity.'

"Often, it has been a visitor from a foreign land who has reminded us of the fragile privileges we enjoy and how tenuously we cling to them. Alexis de Tocqueville was one. Alexandr Solzhenitsyn is another. Now comes Pope John Paul II.

"In Columbia, South Carolina, the pope warned against the continued breakdown of the family. He blamed the breakdown on 'a false notion of individual freedom' and warned Americans to use their freedom wisely.

"'It would be a great tragedy for the entire human family,' said the pope, 'if the United States, which prides itself on its consecration to freedom, were to lose sight of the true meaning of that noble word. America, you cannot insist on the right to choose, without also insisting on the right to choose well, the duty to choose the truth.'

"The pope also said the breakdown had occurred because 'fundamental values, essential to the well-being of individuals, families, and the entire nation, are being emptied of their real content.'

"He is right. Freedom, emptied of its 'real content,' more closely fits the meaning of license: 'freedom that allows or is used with irresponsibility; disregard for rules of personal conduct; licentiousness.'

"The late Bishop Fulton J. Sheen spoke of freedom's limits in 1979: 'Rights are related to personal dignity and identity. . . . But how do we know the identity of anything? By its limits. How do I know the identity of a football field? By its boundaries. How do I know my identity? By my duties, my responsibilities—and they are principally to God, to neighbor, to my country. . . .'

"Our Founders recognized such duties, which must be assumed with a deep sense of responsibility. Fifty-six of them signed the Declaration of Independence, but not all survived to see the Constitution ratified. All paid a price for their commitment to obtain freedom for the common good.

"Nine died in the Revolutionary War. Five were captured by the British and died under torture. Twelve had their homes ransacked and burned to the ground. Dr. John Witherspoon's home and college library were burned. Thomas Keen was forced to move five times in as many months to escape capture. He settled at last in a log cabin on the Susquehanna. Thomas Nelson, Jr., when his home was occupied by British General Charles Cornwallis, urged General George Washington to open fire and destroy his house. He died in poverty.

"The fifty-six had pledged their lives, their honor and liberty. Seventeen of the signers lost everything they had. Many lost their lives, all of them lost their liberty for a time, but none lost his honor. It was because they knew the meaning and purpose of freedom.

"Today, 'freedom' seems to mean the right to abort one's child or to censor certain lofty ideas from the public schools while tolerating the filthiest of pornography as First Amendment-protected speech and press. Conviction in political leaders is seen as 'extremism.' It is thought better to consult the polls to arrive at a bottom-line consensus than to posit firm standards of right and wrong and challenge the nation to follow. Had the Founders behaved similarly, the queen of England would be pictured on our money.

"The United States was founded and the Constitution written on the basis of certain universally held presuppositions. Because those presuppositions are under attack and words like 'freedom' have been, in the pope's words, emptied of their real content, the future is less certain than perhaps at any time since our beginning."

No Greater Guilt

It is true that we get the kind of leadership we deserve. So if we despair over the quality of political, financial, and even religious leadership, is it not possible that those who are corrupt might merely be our own reflections staring back at us from a full-length mirror?

Keith Ablow thinks so. Ablow is a Boston physician who wrote a "Rostrum" column for the 25 January 1988 issue of *U.S. News & World Report.*

Ablow believes that by focusing so much of our attention on presidential candidates and their flaws we avoid focusing on ourselves.

"We give ourselves breaks," says Ablow. "A few too many items in the express checkout at the grocery store, a few padded expense vouchers for income-tax time, a little fib about our car for sale, just one extramarital affair. No one will get hurt. We're human, aren't we?

"We are, and human beings are far from perfect. To be human implies that we will make mistakes. But it's more than that we feel human. We now feel *entitled.* We don't even consider our transgressions to be blunders—we expect them. Some have even become rites of passage—the experimentation with illegal drugs while an undergraduate, the other woman (or other man) during a midlife crisis. Growing up and growing old have somehow come to include growing cynical."

Some say that such things don't matter and that we can categorize certain sins as public or private, as Gary Hart has attempted to do. But Ablow doesn't buy it.

"I think we're paying the price for that kind of slack attitude right now, and the cost will only get higher. Our inattention to the quality of our character has spilled over into inattention to the quality of our work, of our mothering and fathering, of our educational system. The debt gets paid in strange theaters—lack of competitiveness in foreign markets, youngsters who turn to drugs, illiteracy in high-school graduates."

Do you see how all things are inner-connected? Even the trade deficit, brought on by the failure of American products to sell well overseas, can be traced, at least partially, to the crumbling moral foundation of our country. Why work hard? Why produce superior products? Where's the incentive? For whom or for what am I working? For money? Is it in money we now trust rather than in God? Money is soon spent and never satisfies, even when there is some left over.

Ablow specifically rejects the idea so prominent in our culture—that who a person is in private has nothing to do with who he is and what he does in public. That this line of reasoning has gained such wide acceptance, even in the face of considerable evidence to the contrary, is symptomatic of the neutralization of our moral consciousness.

"A truly great society cannot be built even by the most pristine of leaders when the man on the street measures his own character by a lesser standard," says Ablow. "If the spring of idealism and creativity in this country fails to revive, it will not be because one or two or three or more politicians disappoint us. It will be because we disappoint ourselves—maybe without even knowing it, maybe without caring—and continue to lose pride in the kind of people we are."

Postlude

Having been named for the two sons of President Calvin Coolidge (my grandfather and Mrs. Coolidge were first cousins, and John is my first name), I have recently begun reading some of what Coolidge said and wrote while in office. It bears little resemblance to what historians have written about our thirtieth president.

On 5 July 1926, in celebration of the one hundred fiftieth anniversary of the Declaration of Independence, Coolidge delivered a speech in Philadelphia entitled "The Inspiration of the Declaration." In that speech, Coolidge appealed to a standard and an ethic that many Americans have not only forgotten, but seem reluctant to rebuild.

The speech is remarkable for its historical clarity and unapologetic attitude concerning the necessity of positing a unified moral ethic as a condition for maintaining freedom.

In speaking of the thinking that preceded the writing of the Declaration of Independence, Coolidge said, "No one can examine this record and escape the conclusion that in the great outline of its principles the Declaration was the result of the religious teachings of the preceding period. The profound philosophy which Jonathan Edwards applied to theology, the popular preaching of George Whitfield, had aroused the thought and stirred the people of the Colonies in preparation for this great event. No doubt the speculations which had been going on in England, and especially on the Continent, lent their influence to the general sentiment of the times. Of course, the world is always influenced by all the experience and all the thought of the past. But when it comes to a contemplation of the immediate conception of the principles of human relationship which went into the Declaration of Independence we are not required to extend our search beyond our own shores. They are found in the early texts, the sermons, and the writings of the early colonial clergy who were earnestly undertaking to instruct their congregations in the great mystery of how to live. They justified freedom by the text that we are all created in the divine image, all partakers of the divine spirit."

Having established the historical roots of the document, Coolidge went on to warn what will happen if those roots are denied nourishment: "A spring will cease to flow if its source be dried up; a tree will wither if its roots be destroyed. In its main features the Declaration of Independence is a great spiritual document. It is a declaration not of material but of spiritual conceptions. Equality, liberty, popular sovereignty, the rights of man—these are not elements which we can see and touch. They are ideals. They have their source and their roots in the religious convictions. They belong to the unseen world. Unless the faith of the American people in these religious convictions is to endure, the principles of our Declaration will perish. *We can not continue to enjoy the result if we neglect and abandon the cause"* [emphasis mine].

Coolidge could have been issuing a critique of our modern culture when he put into proper order the place of ethics and the role of the state: "Governments do not make ideals, but ideals make governments. This is both historically and logically true. Of course the government can help sustain ideals and can create institutions through which they can be the better observed, but their source by their very nature is in the people. The people have to bear their own responsibilities. There is no method by which that burden can be shifted to the government. *It is not the enactment, but the observance of laws, that creates the character of a nation"* [emphasis mine].

Without apology, Coolidge gave credit where credit was due: "We hold that the duly authorized expression of the will of the people has a divine sanction. But even in that we come back to the theory of John Wise that 'Democracy is Christ's government.' The ultimate sanction of law rests on the righteous authority of the Almighty."

Imagine a political leader saying something like that today. He or she would immediately face a lawsuit from the American Civil Liberties Union for bridging the "wall" supposedly separating church and state.

Coolidge continued to hammer home his point that we cannot have ethics without law or law without God: "Our forefathers came to certain conclusions and decided upon certain courses of action which have been a great blessing to the world. Before we can understand their conclusions we must go back and review the course which they followed. We must think the thoughts which they thought. Their intellectual life centered around the meeting-house. They were intent upon religious worship. While there were always among them men of deep learning, and later those who had comparatively large possessions, the mind of the people was not so much engrossed in how much they knew, or how much they had, as in how they were going to live. While scantily provided with other literature, there was a wide acquaintance with the Scriptures."

There is virtually no acquaintance at all with Scripture today, even among many Christians, and that is a major source of our present difficulties.

Coolidge concluded this line of thinking about the source of the founder's wisdom and strength and, thus, the source of the initial and subsequent strength of the nation: "Over a period as great as that which measures the existence of our independence they were subject to this discipline not only in their religious life and educational training, but also in their political thought. They were a people who came under the influence of a great spiritual development and acquired a great moral power.

"No other theory is adequate to explain or comprehend the Declaration of Independence. It is the product of the spiritual insight of the people. We live in an age of science and of abounding accumulation of material things. These did not create our Declaration. Our Declaration created them. The things of the spirit come first. Unless we cling to that, all our material prosperity, overwhelming though it may appear, will turn to a barren sceptre in our grasp. If we are to maintain the great heritage which has been bequeathed to us, we must be like-minded as the fathers who created it. We must not sink into a pagan materialism. We must cultivate the reverence which they had for the things that are holy. We must follow the spiritual and moral leadership which they showed. We must keep replenished, that they may glow with a more compelling flame, the altar fires before which they worshipped."

Coolidge's forecast of a "barren sceptre" resulting from our failure to adhere to these first principles came true economically in the 1929 stock market crash and resulting Depression, which began three years after this address. Morally, it took another forty years for the barrenness to develop, but can anyone disagree that we now hold such a scepter in our hands?

Sadly, neither the Coolidge speech nor any similar sentiments from our leaders of the past are included in any history textbook used today in American public schools. No wonder so many high school and college students are infected with the virus of relativistic thinking and the multiple side effects that accompany this disease.

Members of the U.S. Senate gather weekly for a prayer breakfast for those who wish to attend. The breakfasts are off the record and are limited to senators. I obtained a transcript of remarks made by Strom Thurmond, Republican senator from South Carolina, at one of these Wednesday gatherings. He spoke on integrity, and his assessment of our nation and his proposals for its restoration are as profound and prophetic as anything I have read.

"I am greatly concerned about this issue [of integrity]," said Thurmond. "For in the gradual erosion of our nation's integrity, I see a tragic crumbling of America's strength. . . .

"Psychologists have offered many reasons for its demise—television and its cynicism; the breakdown of the family and religion; the growing philosophy that all things are relative and that there is no right and wrong; an educational system that emphasizes product rather than process.

"All of these theories are valid, but I think there is still a deeper explanation—and our society has somehow lost its appreciation and understanding of the God who made this nation.

"It does not take much reading in the Scriptures to realize that God values very different things than our society values today. There He says, 'My thoughts are not your thoughts, nor are your ways My ways.'

"He tends to work in a different way than we do today, often using people of integrity and faith rather than those of wealth and power. Consider the manner in which He used a shepherd boy and his slingshot to slay a mighty giant in his armor; tumbled the walls of Jericho with a silent procession of unarmed men, women and children; or the way He used a man who could not speak to lead thousands of Israelites out of Egypt.

"On the other hand, look at the things our nation values—influence, money, triumph, success, intellect, ability. In recent years, our society has focused more and more on results, often trading integrity as if it were another commodity on the marketplace.

"My lifetime has spanned some of the most rapid technological changes in history. I have lived through the first airplane flight and the first step on the moon. I have seen the face of war change from the traditional land and sea tactics to the cosmic threat of nuclear annihilation. I have witnessed the transformation of political campaigns from stump speeches and whistle-stop tours to jet-set schedules and multimillion dollar television ad campaigns.

"I have been fascinated with the technology of this century; yet, I wonder if somehow these very accomplishments have been the beginning of our downfall. Very subtly, we have begun to think that the mind of man can do anything—that nothing is beyond its grasp. The human will has become an all-powerful god, with all things expendable for the sake of its success—especially integrity.

"So how do we address this loss of integrity in our culture? Will it forever take the recurring flash of a *Challenger* explosion or the devastation of an AIDS virus to shake us from our illusion and remind us that we still need something beyond ourselves?

"I desperately hope not, and for a moment now, I want to offer some practical suggestions on ways we, as United States senators, can restore integrity in our society.

"As a first step, I believe we must make a complete shift in our way of thinking, stepping away from the Midas-touched path of our culture and changing our frame of reference so that we value the same things as God.

"In the Holy Scriptures, treasuring integrity is clearly essential to a new way of thinking. The Psalmist says, 'he who walks with integrity' will never be shaken. Proverbs reminds us that 'he who walks with integrity walks securely, but he who perverts his way will be found out.'

"Yet though we ourselves say we value integrity, we often admire success and power more. Unless we can change our mind-set, we too will be encouraging a society that separates spiritual values from 'the real world' and treasures glamour and achievement instead.

"Practically, this new way of thinking might mean taking time away from our largest contributor to visit with a constituent who wants to talk about his social security check. It may mean staying home with our families rather than attending that political dinner. It may mean pausing during a busy day to evaluate the things that are motivating us.

"As a second step, we must accept our need for God, realizing that integrity comes only through His grace. Unless we acknowledge that we can do no good on our own we are living a lie and pretending integrity. Integrity is not something that can be manufactured or performed, but comes only as we admit our weaknesses and recognize our total dependence on God.

"Our founding fathers had a great sense of their dependence and reliance on God. Remember the words of Benjamin Franklin who urged that deadlocked Constitutional Convention to prayer, 'We have been assured, sir, in the sacred Writings, that "except the Lord build the house, they labor in vain that built it." And, if a sparrow cannot fall to the ground without His notice, is it possible that an empire can rise without His aid? The longer I live, the more convincing proofs I see of this truth—that God governs in the affairs of men.' As the current keepers of our nation's flame, we need the same reliance on God.

"Once we have changed our perspective and admitted our need for God, our next step is to surround ourselves with people of integrity. There is a proverb that says, 'He who walks with wise men will be wise, but the companion of fools will be destroyed.' If we surround ourselves with advisors and friends who hold the same values we do, we will be able to be honest with them and ourselves and more likely to maintain our integrity.

"Finally, we must value integrity in others—in our staff members, our families, even among ourselves. How often do we focus on the quality of work our staff members produce instead of the quality of their character? How often do we give our children the impression that we care more about their A's than the integrity of their effort?

"If we can do these four things—change our mind-set, realize our need for God, surround ourselves with people of integrity, and value integrity in others—we will become men and women of integrity. If we can hold integrity in our midst, then these Wednesday meetings will be among the most essential things we do during the week. For what happens here goes far beyond these four walls, into committee meetings, onto the Senate floor, and into the national limelight. 'A little leaven leavens the whole lump,' Scripture says, and if we can build open and honest friendships with one another—friendships not based solely on our performance, but on our love for Christ and our fellow man—we will begin to change the face of this nation. The price we pay for integrity will be great, but I believe it is worth it."

Future generations will not judge this generation of Americans on the extent of our wealth, the power of our military, or the size of our budget deficit. Come to Washington, D.C., and tour the Capitol building. You will not find a single monument erected to any leader because of his or her economic policies.

Lincoln is enshrined in marble and in the hearts of the American people for his courageous and moral stands on matters of principle: the maintenance of the union and the emancipation of slaves.

For what will our generation be remembered one hundred years, five hundred years, a millennium from now?

It certainly will not be for the size of our defense budget. A nation's ultimate strength does not come from arms, as important as they are to deter aggressors. A nation's strength comes from within, from the moral and ethical standards by which a people live.

The decline of those standards has made us vulnerable. Only a return to them will make us strong again.

Appendix & Notes

Appendix

The problem of integrity in government is not new. This has been a common topic for authors and statesmen to discuss since antiquity. For this reason a small selection of quotations on this topic follows in order to put the current discussion about the decline of ethics—both public and private—in perspective. It has long been recognized that there is a relation between public and private integrity and between the violation of public trust and lack of personal integrity. Since the laying of the foundations of Christendom, there has been a commonly accepted standard of Christian ethics for public and personal conduct that has been generally assumed in the Western world. Therefore the references to integrity usually refer to only one aspect of ethics that is under discussion in a particular case. Due to the reality of human depravity and the constant temptations to transgress God's laws (as expressed in the Ten Commandments), there is a constant need to maintain high standards of thought and deed both in public and personal life.

———

The Lives of the Twelve Caesars, written by the first-century Roman historian Suetonius, is a classic study of what happens when public and personal integrity vanish with disastrous consequences for society. He quotes the Emperor Caligula (who ruled Rome from A.D. 37–41) as declaring, "Remember that I have the power to do anything to anybody." Suetonius continues: "Yet even at that time he could not control his natural cruelty and viciousness, but he was a most eager witness of the tortures and executions of those who suffered punishment, revelling [*sic*] at night in gluttony and adultery, disguised in a wig and a long robe." Concerning Nero (who ruled from A.D. 54–68), Suetonius observed: "Although at first his acts of wantonness, lust, extravagance, avarice and cruelty were gradual and secret, and might be condoned as follies of youth, yet even then their nature was such that no one doubted that they were defects of his character and not due to his time of life. . . . Indeed there was no kind of relationship that he did not violate in his career of crime."

"Transported and puffed up with such successes, as he considered them, he boasted that no prince had ever known what power he really had, and he often threw out unmistakable hints that he would not spare even those of the Senate who survived, but would one day blot out the whole order from the State and hand over the rule of the provinces and the command of the armies to the Roman Knights and to his freedmen" (Suetonius, *The Lives of the Twelve Caesars,* ed. Joseph Gavorse [New York: Modern Library, 1959], 185, 172, 257, 265, 267).

———

In 1516, the Christian humanist, Desiderius Erasmus (c. 1466–1536) published a book on *The Education of a Christian Prince.* As one of the foremost thinkers of his age, Erasmus conversed regularly with many rulers and had the opportunity to see them in action at close range. In his book, Erasmus emphasized a program of education for future rulers who would be virtuous princes.

"Therefore, the tutor should first see that his pupil loves and honors virtue as the finest quality of all, the most felicitous, the most fitting a prince; and that he loathes and shuns moral turpitude as the foulest and most terrible of things. Lest the young prince be accustomed to regard riches as an indispensable necessity, to be gained by right or wrong, he should learn that those are not true honors which are commonly acclaimed as such. True honor is that which follows on virtue and right action of its own will; the less affected it is, the more it redounds to fame. The low pleasures of the people are so far beneath a prince, especially a Christian prince, that they hardly become any man. . . .

"Whenever the prince picks up a book, he should do so not with the idea of gaining pleasure but of bettering himself by his reading. He who really wants to do better can easily find the means of becoming better. A great part of goodness is the desire to be good; for example, anyone who knows and hates the disease of political ambition, irascibility, or passionate desire, and opens a book [to find something] by which he may cure his malady, easily finds a remedy that will either remove the cause or [at any rate] lessen it" (Desiderius Erasmus, *The Education of a Christian Prince*, trans. Lester K. Born [New York: Columbia University Press, 1936], 148, 203).

———

The Reformer Martin Luther (1483–1546) looked at the question of integrity in his *Temporal Authority: To What Extent It Should Be Obeyed* in 1523:

"He must give consideration and attention to his subjects, and really devote himself to it. This he does when he directs his every thought to making himself useful and beneficial to them; when instead of thinking, 'the land and people belong to me, I will do what best pleases me,' he thinks rather, 'I belong to the land and the people, I shall do what is useful and good for them. My concern will be not how to lord it over them and dominate them, but how to protect and maintain them in peace and plenty.' He should picture Christ to himself, and say, 'Behold, Christ, the supreme ruler, came to serve me; he did not seek to gain power, estate, and honor from me, but considered only my need, and directed all things to the end that I should gain power, estate, and honor from him and through him. I will do likewise, seeking from my subjects not my own advantage but theirs. I will use my office to serve and protect them, listen to their problems and defend them, and govern to the sole end that they, not I, may benefit and profit from my rule.' In such a manner should a prince in his heart empty himself of his power and authority, and take unto himself the needs of his subjects, dealing with them as though they were his own needs. For this is what Christ did to us (Phil. 2:7); and these are the proper works of Christ love. . . .

"Therefore, we will close with this brief summation, that a prince's duty is fourfold: First, toward God there must be true confidence and earnest prayer; second, toward his subjects there must be love and Christ service; third, with respect to his counselors and officials he must maintain an untrammeled reason and unfettered judgment; fourth, with respect to evildoers he must manifest a restrained severity and firmness. Then the prince's job will be done right, both outwardly and inwardly; it will be pleasing to God and to the people. But he will have to expect much envy and sorrow on account of it; the cross will soon rest on the shoulders of such a prince" (Martin Luther, "The Christian in Society," in *Luther's Works*, ed. Walther I. Brandt, vol. 45 [Philadelphia: Muhlenberg, 1962], 120, 126).

———

The Reverend Samuel Kendall (1753–1814) was pastor of a Congregational church in Weston, Massachusetts. In 1804 he preached an election sermon on Deut. 32:46–47 that was typical of the early years of the Republic when public conduct and private morality were rightly seen as of one piece.

"Religion and virtue, we infer, . . . will be a prominent feature in the character of wise and good rulers. These are important qualifications for their stations. To concede the general utility of such a principle of action, and yet suppose it unnecessary that rulers should be under its influence, is too great an inconsistency to be seriously maintained. The piety and virtue requisite for the preservation of the body politic ought to be visible in the head. If this be sick, the whole heart will faint. Void of religious principle, or sense of moral obligation, can we believe that civil rulers will be the ministers of God for good? May we not rather apprehend that they will be an encouragement to evil doers, and a terror to those who do well? But a steady eye to a presiding Deity, with humble reliance on the wisdom of his providence, will direct, animate and support them in all the duties of their office, make them faithful, and render them superior to the trials that may await them" (Charles S. Hyneman and Donald S. Lutz, eds., *American Political Writing during the Founding Era, 1760–1805* [Indianapolis: Liberty Press, 1983], 2:1254–55).

———

The Federalist Papers, the classic commentary on the U.S. Constitution written by Alexander Hamilton, James Madison, and John Jay and published in 1787–88, had some optimistic words about the process by which the president of the United States is elected. Wrote Hamilton in "Number 68":

"This process of election affords a moral certainty that the office of President will seldom fall to the lot of any man who is not in an eminent degree endowed with the requisite qualifications. Talents for low intrigue, and the little arts of popularity, may alone suffice to elevate a man to the first honors in a single State; but it will require other talents, and a different kind of merit, to establish him in the esteem and confidence of the whole Union, or of so considerable a portion of it as would be necessary to make him a successful candidate for the distinguished office of President of the United States. It will not be too strong to say that there will be a constant probability of seeing the station filled by characters pre-eminent for ability and virtue. And this will be thought no inconsiderable recommendation of the Constitution by those who are able to estimate the share which the executive in every government must necessarily have in its good or ill administration" (Alexander Hamilton, James Madison, and John Jay, *The Federalist Papers,* ed. Clinton Rossiter [New York: New American Library, 1961], 414).

———

On September 19, 1796, President George Washington delivered his famous Farewell Address, which has become a key document in American history, that suggests the greatness of our first chief executive's character.

"Of all the dispositions and habits which lead to political prosperity, Religion and morality are indispensable supports. In vain would that man claim the tribute of Patriotism, who should labour to subvert these great Pillars of human happiness, these firmest props of the duties of Men and citizens. The mere Politician, equally with the pious man ought to respect and to cherish them. A volume could not trace all their connections with private and public felicity. Let it be simply asked where is the security for property, for reputation, for life, if the sense of religious obligation desert the oaths, which are the instruments of investigation in Courts of Justice? And let us with caution indulge the supposition, that morality can be maintained without religion. Whatever may be conceded to the influence of refined education on minds of peculiar structure, reason and experience both forbid us to expect that National morality can prevail in exclusion of religious principle.

"'Tis substantially true, that virtue or morality is a necessary spring of popular government. The rule indeed extends with more or less force to every species of free Government. Who that is a sincere friend to it, can look with indifference upon attempts to shake the foundations of the fabric" (George Washington, *Basic Writings of George Washington,* ed. Saxe Commins [New York: Random House, 1948], 637).

———

British Prime Minister William Gladstone (1809–98) was an example of the Christian statesman of the nineteenth century. He served as prime minister four times between 1868 and 1894 and sought to have his life reflect high Christian ideals. On July 15, 1869, he noted in his diary that a letter had come "from Mr. Spurgeon (as often from others), an assurance of the prayers of the nonconformists. I think in these and other prayers lies the secret of the strength of body which has been given me in unusual measure during this very trying year" (John Morley, *The Life of William Ewart Gladstone* [New York: Macmillan, 1911] 1:6:272).

Gladstone wrote on December 28, 1872: "Be it however, what it may be, we politicians are children playing with toys in comparison to that great work of and for manhood, which has to be done, and will yet be done, in restoring belief" (Ibid., 2:7:524).

A few years later the great evangelist Charles H. Spurgeon wrote to Gladstone with words of encouragement:

"I felt ready to weep when you were treated with so much contumely by your opponent in your former struggle; and yet I rejoiced that you were educating this nation to believe in conscience and truth. . . . I wish I could brush away the gadflies, but I suppose by this time you have been stung so often that the system has become invulnerable. . . . [Y]ou are loved by hosts of us as intensely as you are hated by certain of the savage party" (Ibid., 2:7:530).

As the prime minister was preparing to visit Spurgeon, the evangelist wrote him in January 1882:

"I feel like a boy who is to preach with his father to listen to him. I shall try not to know that you are there at all, but just preach to my poor people the simple word which has held them by their thousands these twenty-eight years. You do not know how those of us regard you, who feel it a job to live when a premier believes in righteousness. We believe in no man's infallibility, but it is restful to be sure of one man's integrity" (Ibid., 2:7:531).

A recent biographer, Philip Magnus, characterized Gladstone:

"Gladstone's heart was not in politics, which he had chosen early as his field of action from motives with which he was never wholly satisfied. He had resolved, as far as possible, to make politics conform with the highest Christian ethic. He was conscious of the possession of great gifts, and he loved power for the opportunities which it gives; but all his affections were centred upon the universal Christian society, and not upon any local temporal kingdom. After he had abandoned his exalted theory of a union between Church and State, he was content to see the Church become a voluntary body. But the problem of the right relationship between two societies—the one, eternal and divine; the other, mortal and mundane—which has troubled the conscience of Europe for two thousand years, continued to torment Gladstone and to plunge his mind into a seething ferment of restlessness. Throughout the ages, the parties to that ancient dispute have constantly shifted their positions, and Gladstone also shifted his own position. The increasing secularization of nineteenth-century thought made him desist from the intellectual search for a unifying principle. He continued, however, to thirst for it emotionally, pending the full conversion of the leading nations of mankind to the Christian way of life" (Philip Magnus, *Gladstone* [New York: E. P. Dutton, 1954], 440).

———

A similar sense of the positive moral influence of the Christian statesman is seen in the career of Prime Minister Abraham Kuyper (1837–1920) of the Netherlands. In a speech to Parliament in The Hague on December 6, 1902, Kuyper declared:

"It is the intention of the government to retard and as much as possible to break the demonic influences which are corroding our national life—drunkenness, the passion for gambling, the open violation of chastity and pornography. I will go into this matter no further. . . . [I]t is the intention of the government to affirm in legislation the Christian foundations long rooted in our history which are now being eroded: authority, family, marriage and the churches" (Abraham Kuyper, *Parlementaire Redevoeringen, II, Ministerielle Redevoeringen, Tweede Kamer, I* [Amsterdam: Van Holkema & Warendorf, n.d.], 251; trans. McKendree R. Langley).

In order to dispel any concern that his was a theocratic program, Kuyper insisted his was a pluralist philosophy of democratic consensus building in a speech on December 5, 1901:

"We do not examine anyone's faith nor act as heresy-hunters seeking to prove the unbelief of our fellow citizens. For us the only question . . . is this: Who stands with us in upholding a common political conviction on the basis of Scripture?" (Quoted in McKendree R. Langley, *The Practice of Political Spirituality* [Ontario: Paideia Press, 1984], 76).

———

The high standards of President Woodrow Wilson formed the basis of much of the political idealism of the twentieth century. The following statements bear this out. The first is from a speech given at a YMCA convention in Pittsburgh on October 24, 1914. The second is from his Second Inaugural Address of March 4, 1917.

"That means that eternal vigilance is the price, not only of liberty, but of a great many other things. It is the price of everything that is good. It is the price of one's own soul. It is the price of the souls of the people you love; and when it comes down to the final reckoning you have a standard that is immutable. What shall a man give in exchange for his soul? Will he sell that? Will he consent to see another man sell his soul? Will he consent to see the conditions of his community such that men's souls are debauched and trodden underfoot in the mire? What shall he give in exchange for his own soul, or any other man's soul? And since the world, the world of affairs, the world of society, is nothing less and nothing more than all of us put together, it is a great enterprise for the salvation of the soul in this world as well as in the next. There is a text in Scripture that has always interested me profoundly. It says godliness is profitable in this life as well as in the life that is to come; and if you do not start it in this life, it will not reach the life that is to come. Your measurements, your directions, your whole momentum, have to be established before you reach the next world. This world is intended as the place in which we shall show that we know how to grow in the stature of manliness and of righteousness."

"I stand here and have taken the high and solemn oath to which you have been audience because the people of the United States have chosen me for this august delegation of power and have by their gracious judgment named me their leader in affairs. I know now what the task means. I realize to the full the responsibility which it involves. I pray God I may be given the wisdom and the prudence to do my duty in the true spirit of this great people. I am their servant and can succeed only as they sustain and guide me by their confidence and their counsel. The thing I shall count upon, the thing without which neither counsel nor action will avail, is the unity of America,—an America united in feeling, in purpose, and in its vision of duty, of opportunity, and of service. We are to beware of all men who would turn the tasks and the necessities of the Nation to their own private profit or use them for the building up of private power; beware that no faction or disloyal intrigue break the harmony or embarrass the spirit of our people; beware that our Government be kept pure and incorrupt in all its parts. United alike in the conception of our duty and in the high resolve to perform it in the face of all men, let us dedicate ourselves to the great task to which we must now set our hand. For myself I beg your tolerance, your countenance, and your united aid. The shadows that now lie dark upon our path will soon be dispelled and we shall walk with the light all about us if we be but true to ourselves,—to ourselves as we have wished to be known in the counsels of the world and in the thought of all those who love liberty and justice and the right exalted" (George M. Harper, *President Wilson's Addresses* [New York: Henry Holt, 1918] 116, 240).

———

Konrad Adenauer (1876–1967) served as the first postwar chancellor of West Germany (1949–63). He was largely responsible for the remarkable rebirth of that nation. As a Christian Democrat he had some strong convictions about integrity.

"A large number of people who thought as I did believed that only a new party based on the broadest Christian foundations, on firm ethical principles, and able to draw on all strata of the German electorate, would be in a position to re-animate Germany.

"The National Socialists had opened our eyes to the power wielded by a dictatorial state. I had seen the atrocities of

National Socialism, the consequences of dictatorship. I had lost the vocation to which I had devoted my life; my wife was hopelessly ill as a result of a stay in the Gestapo prison at Brauweiler. I had seen the consequences of the war. Three of my sons had served at the front and I had suffered constant anxiety for them; one of them had been severely wounded.

"I had heard about the crimes committed against Jews and by Germans against their fellow-Germans. I had seen where an atheistic dictatorship could lead. I had seen Germany plunged into chaos.

"From the East we were menaced by an atheist, communist dictatorship, the Soviet Union showed us that a dictatorship of the Left is at least as dangerous as one of the Right. As a result of the war the Soviet Union had advanced deep into central Germany, up to the Elbe, and was [a] great danger to us.

"We had seen in the National Socialist state, and we saw again in Communist Russia, the dangers inherent in a party that disregarded ethical principles. This convinced most of the adherents of the former Centre, and many members of the former parties of the Right, of the necessity for us to unite into a new party founded on an ethical basis.

"The conviction began to spread that only a great party with its roots in Christian-Western thinking and ethics could educate the German people for their resurgence, and build a strong dyke [sic] against the atheist dictatorship of communism" (Konrad Adenauer, *Memoirs, 1945–1953* [Chicago: Henry Regnery, 1966], 44–45).

———

Another major Christian Democratic statesmen from the same early postwar period was Robert Schuman (1886–1963) of France. He served as his country's premier from 1947–48 and then as foreign minister from 1948–52. He was the political father of the European Coal and Steel Community that broke the pattern of centuries of hostility between France and

Germany by initiating the politics of reconciliation that lay at the heart of the European Common Market.

His biographer, Robert Rochefort, wrote:

"Robert Schuman can be seen in a purely political sense: the importance of his work on European matters would by itself justify the undertaking. As the greatest foreign minister in a generation, the history of his ministerial contribution is yet to be written. But we have a different purpose: it is Robert Schuman himself that we want to portray . . . , that this statesman of stature was also a 'man of good will' who dedicated his life to 'doing good' in the Christian sense of the term. In all circumstances he was a man of meditation and prayer, excluding in principle from both his public and private life all recourse to unethical means to achieving goals. . . .

"He remained a spiritual man in the midst of his public life living out the same ethic in the solitude of his estate of Scy-Chazelles, in the Gestapo prison and in governmental offices. He played a major role on the world scene without departing from either humility or neighborly love. . . .

"Was there a contradiction in him between public life and private life? He did not think so and his success affirmed his view. . . .

"He understood that statesmen like humanity in general should seek to be an instrument of Providence to carry out His goals. Public or private, his life was a unity with no ulterior motives and no scheming. . . . [He was] the statesman who at the end of a public career full of important accomplishments affirmed 'one should never lie, not even in politics'" (Robert Rochefort, *Robert Schuman* [Paris: Cerf, 1968], 10–12; trans. McKendree R. Langley).

In his memoirs Schuman wrote:

"The task of the responsible statesman is to reconcile these two orders of consideration—the sacred and the profane—in a synthesis both delicate and necessary. . . .

"From the beginning Christ was opposed to fanaticism when he submitted to become the victim in noble fashion. His Kingdom was not of this world. This signifies that Christian civilization should not be the product of an immediate, violent revolution but of a progressive transformation and a patient education with the greatest principles of love, sacrifice and humility which are the foundations of the new society" (Robert Schuman, *Pour l'Europe* [Paris: Nagel, 1964], 65–66).

———

President Herbert Hoover had his share of difficulty in office most often associated with the Great Depression yet he maintained high standards in the White House. He referred to the problem of integrity first at the dedication of the Warren Harding Memorial and then in reference to his own appointees at the cabinet and subcabinet levels.

"Warren Harding had a dim realization that he had been betrayed by a few of the men whom he had trusted, by men who he had believed were his devoted friends. It was later proved in the courts of the land that these men had betrayed not alone the friendship and trust of their staunch and loyal friend but they had betrayed their country. That was the tragedy of the life of Warren Harding.

"There are disloyalties and there are crimes which shock our sensibilities, which may bring suffering upon those who are touched by their immediate results. But there is no disloyalty and no crime in all the category of human weakness which compares with the failure of probity in the conduct of public trust. Monetary loss or even the shock of moral sensibilities is perhaps a passing thing, but the breaking down of the faith of a people in the honesty of their government and in the integrity of their institutions, the lowering of respect for the standards of honor which prevail in high places, are crimes for which punishment can never atone. . . .

"I doubt if any President was ever surrounded by men and

women of more personal loyalty or devotion to public service than this group. Had the Republican party remained in power, they were the young men who could have carried the highest traditions of public service. We of course did not always agree, but we searched out solutions without public debates or rancor.

"There are three tributes that can be given to them all: First, there has never been substantiated challenge to the integrity of any one of them; we had no scandals, no misfeasance whatever in the administration. Second, no one of them in whom I imposed trust and confidence has ever defamed my actions or even criticized them in after life. Third, every man or woman in the group has given me ever afterwards lasting friendship and loyalty. For all of which I owe them an unpayable debt" (Herbert Hoover, *The Memoirs of Herbert Hoover: The Cabinet and the Presidency, 1920–1933* [New York: Macmillan, 1952], 53, 221).

———

President Dwight D. Eisenhower was also concerned with ethics in and out of government as he related in the second volume of his memoirs:

"In any case, we knew what we faced at the time and acted accordingly.

"Many things have happened since the day I left the Presidency on January 20, 1961. Intensely interesting to me are those that bear some relation to, or were affected by, the decisions and actions of my two administrations.

"Without delving extensively into political happenings and trends since I returned to private life—they may be the subject of other writings, perhaps—I cannot avoid some mention of problems, continuing or emerging, that cause me as deep concern as they did in the days when I bore the responsibilities of the Presidency. Most of these, it seems, revolve around one profound question: Will a great self-governing people such as ours—a people that in three and a half centuries converted a vast wilderness into the richest and most powerful political grouping on earth—continue to practice, in affluence, the pioneering virtues and be guided by the moral values that in leaner times brought us, by the middle of the twentieth century, to an unparalleled pinnacle of power?

"To pose this question suggests another, possibly more meaningful one: Do we see signs, even now, that point to a weakening among our people of the qualities of moral courage, determination, self-reliance, venturesomeness, and ambitions to excel, so constantly noted by past writers of the American saga?

"Communications media bring to us sickening and depressing accounts of deliberate lawlessness, arrogant selfishness, disloyalty, laxity in conduct, and all kinds of downright wickedness. Worse, when learning of these things, we seem to have lost some of our capacity for honesty and righteous indignation.

"A reckless driver, personally responsible for a serious accident, has his license suspended for a few weeks. The number of divorces goes steadily upward. A movie star becomes a drug addict, another leads a loose and lascivious life, and both become 'hotter' box office attractions than before.

"The electorate of a city chooses as its mayor a man serving a jail sentence; churches and homes are bombed; innocent children pay with broken bodies, sometimes with their lives, for the hate and prejudice that lighted the fuses. Witnesses to a murder refuse to 'get involved' either by assisting the victim or helping the police.

"Such things would provide little cause for comment if they were isolated instances of the presence among us of individuals with psychopathic tendencies. When they are reported regularly as normal occurrences throughout the land, and we seemingly accept them as just 'human nature,' the situation has sinister implications.

"The real question for each of us then becomes: 'Am I

doing my duty as a citizen?' For certain it is that if every
decent person in this nation would arouse his own conscience, help elect to public office persons of proved courage
and integrity, support vocally and morally his police force,
his corps of teachers, the local judges and the lawmakers
and their governors in state capitals, soon the numerous
newspaper accounts of such crimes, delinquencies, and neglect would decline. And each of us would once again stand
straight and proud, proud of himself, his children, and the
community in which he lives" (Dwight D. Eisenhower, *The
White House Years: Waging Peace, 1956–1961* [Garden City,
N.Y.: Doubleday, 1965], 655–56).

————

Daniel R. Coats, a congressman from Indiana and a member of the Select Committee on Children, Youth, and Families
of the One Hundreth Congress, recently added the following
to the debate on ethics:

"The character of a candidate should embody a high sense
of integrity, values and conviction. He or she should demonstrate good management of personal affairs since a candidate
is a role model for others who trust him. But Christian politicians are not better than others—all are sinners saved by
grace. The key factor is how he handles his mistakes and that
involves his character and Christian values. Christian politicians must be careful with Christian rhetoric in campaigns.
Some hypocritically espouse values they don't live by or believe in simply because such views are popular.

"Today there is much public discussion of the personal
finances, spouse and family life of candidates. The press
is struggling with the proper way to do this. It is hard for a
candidate to go through an examination of his family life and
past. In this public examination his life becomes an open
book. Every candidate must be willing to undergo this process. But the scrutiny must be fair in emphasizing how the

examination will affect the candidate's ability to do his job. . . .

"Christians differ on [whether or not morality is a public issue]. It is important to question candidates about moral issues. Yet we must remember that there are those of integrity and Christian faith on both sides of many such questions. We must approach the areas of public morality with humility.

"Evangelicals have become more involved in the political process on moral issues since 1980. I credit President Jimmy Carter with legitimizing Christian faith in public life much more than previously. But an election involves both a candidate and the supportive staff. Unfortunately Carter had many staffers who did not share his values. For example, there were disturbing stories of the questionable moral behavior of some of his staff. This hurt Carter. Carter was part of the trend back to traditional values in public life that included both evangelicals and fundamentalists, but it didn't get beyond the presidency. Since 1980 this trend spread to the Congress and has become more pervasive" ("Look for Competence, Coats Counsels Voters," *Eternity Magazine* 39 [April 1988]:23–24).

Notes

Chapter 1
Hart's Desire

1. *The New York Times,* 2 August 1987.
2. *The New York Times,* 5 April 1987.
3. *The Washington Times,* 20 September 1987.
4. *The Washington Post,* 20 September 1987.
5. *Perspective* 39 no. 15.

Chapter 2
Pinkie Rings and Heavenly Things

1. By special permission of Leona Jay Music, Inc. (Chet Atkins-Margaret Archer © 1987).

Chapter 3
Fools and Their Money

1. Ken Auletta, *Greed and Glory on Wall Street: The Fall of the House of Lehman* (New York: G. K. Hall, 1987), 234.
2. Ibid., 246.
3. Ibid., 247.
4. Ibid., 250.

Chapter 4
Roaring Back to the Future

1. Frederick Lewis Allen, *Only Yesterday: An Informal History of the Nineteen-Twenties* (New York: Blue Ribbon Books, 1931), 94–95.
2. Ibid., 103.
3. Warren G. Harding, *Last Speeches of Warren G. Harding Delivered on His Alaskan Tour, June to August 1923* (Washington, D.C.: U.S. Senate, 1923), 110.
4. Ibid., 23.
5. Ibid., 109.
6. Ibid., 213.
7. Ibid., 215.
8. Ibid.
9. Ibid., 338.
10. Ibid., 393.
11. Andrew Sinclair, *The Available Man: The Life Behind the Masks of Warren Gamaliel Harding* (New York: Macmillan, 1965), 288; see also Francis Russell, *The Shadow of Blooming Grove: Warren G. Harding and His Times* (New York: McGraw-Hill, 1968).
12. Russell, *The Shadow of Blooming Grove*, 168–69.
13. Ibid., 310–11.
14. Ibid., 419.
15. Clarence Darrow, *The Story of My Life* (New York:

Scribner's, 1932), 249; see also Ray Ginger, *Six Days or Forever* (Boston: Beacon, 1958).

16. Quoted in George M. Marsden, *Fundamentalism and American Culture* (New York: Oxford University Press, 1980), 187.

17. Quoted in ibid., 187–88.

18. Ibid.

19. Nancy B. Mavity, *Sister Aimee* (Garden City, N.Y.: Doubleday/Doran, 1931), 336; see also Lately Thomas, *The Vanishing Evangelist* (New York: Viking, 1959).

20. Lewis, *Only Yesterday*, 338.

21. William S. Myers and Walter H. Newton, *The Hoover Administration: A Documented Narrative* (New York: Scribner's, 1936), 23.

22. *Philadelphia Inquirer*, 21 October 1987.

23. Herbert Hoover, *The Memoirs of Herbert Hoover: The Great Depression, 1929–1941* (New York: Macmillan, 1952), 19.

24. Arthur M. Schlesinger, Jr., *The Age of Roosevelt: The Crisis of the Old Order, 1919–1933* (Boston: Houghton Mifflin, 1957), 161.

25. Quoted in ibid., 160.

26. Ibid.

Chapter 6
Down Come Baby and All

1. "The Culture of Apathy," *The New Republic*, 8 February 1988, 7–8.

Chapter 7
To Thine Own Self Be True

1. Quoted in McKendree R. Langley, "God and Liberty: The Catholic Quest for Democratic Pluralism from Lamennais to Vatican II," *Pro Rege* (June 1980):16.

2. On Felicite Lamennais, see also F. Lamennais, *Des Progrès de la Révolution et de la Guerre Contre l'Eglise* (Louvain: Vanlinthout et Vandenzande, 1829); Peter N. Stearns, *Priest and Revolutionary: Lamennais and the Dilemma of French Catholicism* (New York: Harper, 1967); John J. Oldfield, *The Problem of Tolerance and Social Existence in the Writings of Felicite Lamennais* (Leiden: E. J. Brill, 1973); Georges Hourdin, *Lamennais: Prophète et Combattant de la Liberté* (Paris: Perrin, 1982); on Abraham Kuyper, see also L. W. G. Scholten, ed., *Dr. A. Kuyper, Gedenkboek, 1837–1937* (Kampen, The Netherlands: J. H. Kok, 1937); McKendree R. Langley, *The Practice of Political Spirituality: Episodes from the Public Career of Abraham Kuyper, 1879–1918* (Ontario: Paideia, 1984); idem, "The Kuyper Memorial: An Evangelical Birthday," *Eternity* 39 (January 1988):16.

Chapter 8
Nothing But the Truth

1. Allan Bloom, *The Closing of the American Mind* (New York: Simon and Schuster, 1987), 60.
2. Ibid., 61.